The Machine That Could

PNGV, A GOVERNMENT-INDUSTRY PARTNERSHIP

Robert M. Chapman

Prepared for the U.S. Department of Commerce

CRITICAL TECHNOLOGIES INSTITUTE

RAND

elements of all three of these situations, but in no clear-cut measure. Thus, when we contemplate how we might produce the shift in product and process technologies necessary to address these issues, we find ourselves in very unfamiliar territory indeed. In essence, we are engaged in a new and bold experiment: Can a collaborative government-industry partnership really provide the benefits we seek and solve the problems that concern us? How can we make it work? What role is most effective for the government? What is the most effective way to partner with the private sector?

This challenge is different from many we have successfully faced in the past. For example, although it deals with technology, it bears little relationship to a "moon shot" type of program. While it appeals to the element in our culture that almost instinctively turns to technology as a solution, simply developing and building a vehicle that performs to specifications and then declaring success would ignore the need for the market and its consumers to make the final determination of success or failure. The market test also requires that the private sector be involved in a manner that differs from the government-contractor relationship that has characterized technology development efforts in the past. A genuine partnership with balanced contributions and leadership roles seems to offer more promise. It is also largely untested.

The times and the newness of the enterprise itself impose constraints: Grand experiments that do not have access to unlimited resources are expected to produce results far superior to the status quo, and they often bring together unfamiliar partners and great challenges. PNGV is no exception; its challenges include the following:

- the difficulty of matching the low manufacturing costs that current technologies have achieved through 100 years of experience with existing processes and materials

- the consequent difficulty of matching the price-performance relationship that already provides incredible value to consumers

- the need for the government to operate initially with a "virtual" budget and rely on nonfiscal policy tools, such as its convening authority and its ability to raise issues with the body politic

- partners—the government and the auto industry—who have not worked together in such a cooperative manner except during times of war.

PNGV seeks potential public benefits and, at the same time, seeks to meet the demands of the market. Further, it must operate within the constraints by using scientific and engineering knowledge in a grand experiment involving both government and industry.

We do not yet know whether PNGV will be successful, although there are encouraging indications. We do not yet know whether the country will decide that this approach is compatible with our view of how a free market should function and that it is useful in solving similar problems facing our society. But if it is judged to be successful and does hold promise for future problems, we will very much want to know the lessons we have learned in how to make such a partnership work and when it is applicable.

Hence this report.

Bruce W. Don
Director, Critical Technologies Institute

The desire to explore the significance of the Partnership for a New Generation of Vehicles (PNGV) and to document its "lessons learned" from a government-management standpoint led the U.S. Department of Commerce (DoC) to request this report. The hope is that the experience gained from government and industry working together to achieve a technical goal may be applied productively to other such partnerships in the future. Further, if this experiment is successful, it may be that other societal objectives may be achieved by government and industry acting similarly in partnership as an alternative to mandates or regulations.

This report discusses the lessons from the first, organizing, phase of PNGV that might guide those embarking on similar partnerships in the future. These lessons are presented in this report as distillations of views of participants in the PNGV, primarily but not exclusively on the government side. This account by the government's first technical manager of the PNGV was developed from notes, recollections, and interviews with former colleagues. Certain observations are presented that represent personal opinions of the author.

This report was written in coordination with a doctoral dissertation by David Trinkle of the RAND Graduate School. His analysis of the PNGV, also supported by the DoC, will be completed in 1998.

There are several other relevant reports on the PNGV. The origins of the PNGV are described comprehensively in a Kennedy School of Government of Harvard University case study (Bunten, 1997). The organizations involved in the partnership and their roles are described in Hillebrand (1996) for SAE. Numerous articles in the automotive trade press have reported various aspects of the program.[1] The technologies the partnership considered prospects for inclusion in the so-called "Super Car" or "Clean Car" expected to result from the program are discussed in a series of bulletins by the U.S. Council for Automotive Research.[2]

CTI was created in 1991 by an act of Congress. It is a federally funded research and development center sponsored by the National Science Foundation and managed by RAND, a nonprofit corporation created for the purpose of improving public policy. CTI's mission is to help improve public policy by conducting objective, independent research and analysis on policy issues which involve science and technology in order to

- Support the Office of Science and Technology Policy and other Executive Branch agencies, offices and councils,
- Help science and technology decisionmakers understand the likely consequences of their decisions and choose among alternative policies, and
- Improve understanding in both the public and private sectors of the ways in which science and technology can better serve national objectives.

CTI research focuses on problems of science and technology policy that involve multiple agencies. In carrying out its mission CTI consults broadly with representatives from private industry, institutions of higher education, and other nonprofit institutions.

Inquiries regarding CTI or this document may be directed to:

Bruce Don
Director, Critical Technologies Institute
RAND
1333 H ST., N.W.
Washington, D.C. 20005
Phone: (202) 296-5000
Web: http://www.rand.org/centers/cti/
Email: cti@rand.org

---

[1] Selected quotations from these reports appear in the appendix.

[2] The council's *Mileposts* is published quarterly.

CONTENTS

FIGURES AND TABLE

Figure

Table

The PNGV represents a groundbreaking approach to U.S. government–industry technological collaboration for the national interest. Several serious societal problems are being addressed, most prominently the impact of the automobile on the environment. The partners—the government and the U.S. domestic automobile industry—have embarked on an enterprise that, if successful, will lead to an "environmentally friendly," affordable, and safe family sedan able to travel 80 miles on a gallon of gas. The industry has committed itself to completing production prototypes of these sedans by the year 2004. The government, for its part, has agreed to make the relevant technologies available to the industry, as well as to provide technical support through the resources of the national laboratories. Thus, the traditional pattern of government–automobile industry relations has taken a new turn. With this partnership, the participants have been able to rise above past acrimony associated with government's perceived intrusion into the marketplace and industry's alleged lack of responsiveness to issues of public concern.

At this point, less than halfway to the final goal of a "Super Car" production prototype, there have been several significant accomplishments that bode well for the ultimate success of the partnership. As a result, there is a recognition that the partnership promises to be a model for how the government may support a technology-intensive industry's response to societal problems without resorting to regulatory actions. Therefore, it will be important to understand the management philosophy, procedures, and reasoning that created an environment for developing technology successfully.

The purpose of this report is to describe the government-side management of the transfer of technology and other technical support of the industry. The study considers PNGV relative only to other cooperative efforts between industry and government that go beyond the traditional models of interaction—regulations or federal contracts. Furthermore, the focus is on partnerships that promote the development and implementation of new technologies.

FEATURES OF THE PARTNERSHIP

Several features of the partnership have enabled progress toward attainment of the ultimate goals. The following are the principal features:

- A clear, easily understood primary goal: a car that gets 80 miles per gallon

- Strong support and leadership at the highest levels of the administration

- The ability to draw on the substantial technical resources within the federal laboratories

- Eager, highly motivated industry partners

- Strong public interest and support.

Conversely, problems have been encountered that continue to pose difficulties: These are related to the voluntary nature of the commitment among the various participants, a lack of interim metrics or checkpoints, the lack of a central budget, the large number of parties involved, and a relatively inflexible plan.

To circumvent these problems and capitalize on the PNGV's advantages, the government side of the partnership adopted a management approach that included organizing, planning, implementing, communicating, and coordinating within the government, as well as with industry, to effect the transfer of technologies. Specific aspects of the government management include the following:

- Establishing a working relationship with participating government agencies, as well as with the automobile industry

- Enlisting high-level support in both government and industry by recruiting top officials

- Starting quickly by utilizing existing funding mechanisms

- Subsuming related government research activities

- Having industry assume the technical lead

- Analyzing components of the problem to set priorities

- Pursuing technologies in parallel and in competition with each other

- Facilitating technology transfer

- Maintaining open communications among participants

- After a period of evaluation, selecting the most promising technologies for incorporation in concept or experimental vehicles

- Subjecting the entire process to annual peer reviews by the National Research Council.

LESSONS LEARNED

Many experiences of the PNGV appear to have relevance for future government-industry partnerships. Highlights of these lessons include the following:

Structuring a Partnership

- Clear and simply stated goals are most effective for motivating technical personnel and winning public support.

- High-level support is vital, within both government and industry.

- Accountability at a high political level in each participating agency is a must.

- Large government-industry partnerships can be more effective if they are limited in number so that resources are not dispersed.

- Means must be found to surmount problems associated with the lack of a central budget.

- The government must anticipate funding and technology needs at the outset and move more expeditiously.

- Outside the core program, projects should be structured to be "dual use."

- It is helpful to build the partnership around an existing core government research and development program.

Social and Cultural Considerations

- Although government and industry may agree to pursue the same goals, it should be expected that the agenda may vary.

- Competition in industry is a stronger force than cooperation and should be channeled rather than discouraged.

- Social encounters improve working-level technical interactions.

- Technical people should be sheltered from political turbulence.

External Aspects

- Program managers must take sufficient time to involve Congress without encouraging micromanagement.

- Public affairs should be given priority as an extremely important component of a government-industry partnership.

- Flexibility and proper planning will help when the partnership is faced with the inevitable unexpected circumstances.

OTHER OBSERVATIONS

In addition to the lessons that might apply to other partnerships, there are also other observations that are more specific to PNGV, including the following:

- The auto industry faces a dynamic technical environment.

- Denying the significance of advancing technology is a peril.

- The uniqueness of the automotive industry should not be a shelter from nontraditional solutions.

- Traditional technologies are unlikely to satisfy the PNGV's goals.

- Feedback from the international automotive arena in reaction to the PNGV has amplified the momentum of technology advancement.

- All indications point to enduring collaborative relationships between the government and the domestic automobile industry through which advanced technologies are applied to make vehicles environmentally friendly and fuel efficient.

- As a "partner" to industry, government can pose a challenge and vice versa.

CONCLUDING THOUGHTS

A government-industry partnership needs constant attention and support to succeed. This entails close oversight of technical developments, their trends, and their significance; attending to congressional and public relations; developing and maintaining relationships with participating government agencies and with the industry partners; and nurturing personal relationships with key people in the partnership. As a minimum, a cooperative, problem-solving environment should be expected. However, in an environment like that engendered by the PNGV, much more is possible. From the interactions between firms came business deals and other new ventures. And even within the government, there were program realignments. These should be viewed as positive developments relative to the broader goals of the PNGV. All this can make the partnership a rewarding experience for all concerned—the government, the industry, and the individuals involved.

To some extent, the PNGV has already succeeded, if success can be measured by the imitation among foreign competitors, some of whom are now striving similarly to introduce new technology to motor vehicles. The United States therefore is in a race it created but in which it must maintain the tempo or see its lead lost.

The encouragement and support of my former government PNGV colleagues are gratefully acknowledged. They generously took the time to give the draft of this report a thorough review. Their comments and helpful suggestions have materially improved the cogency of the report by sharpening the analysis of the instructive aspects of the PNGV.

A special notice is given to Mary L. Good, former Under Secretary for Technology, DoC, and my boss while I was there. Her strong direction of the PNGV and support of the technical effort were instrumental in ensuring a solid foundation and continuing positive outlook for the partnership. It was at her suggestion that my briefing materials on "Lessons Learned from the PNGV" were expanded into this report.

The number of key participants in the PNGV, on both the government and industry sides, is too great to list them all here. However, my most important collaborator must be cited: Pandit G. Patil, Director of the Advanced Vehicle Technologies Office, DoE. He was a source of consistent support with his own time and the resources of his organization.

Although this report is fundamentally a story about how the PNGV functioned from the government perspective, there is no intention to diminish the critically important contributions of the many industry participants. The PNGV directors, in particular, were day-to-day collaborators. The credit for the material successes the program has achieved and will achieve must go primarily to them.

The support of organizations outside the partnership was instrumental to the functioning of the PNGV Secretariat in the Department of Commerce. SAE and the Engineering Society of Detroit (ESD) were especially supportive and generous in arranging resident fellows. To date, there have been four fellows, each serving a one-year term. They were sponsored by the societies and were provided by General Motors, Ford, and Chrysler in sequence. All have been of high technical caliber and have been a substantial resource for the secretariat. The SAE and ESD have additionally sponsored meetings, symposia, and other technical exchanges to assist the PNGV to advance its technical agenda. Max E. Rumbaugh, Jr., the Executive Vice President of the SAE, was instrumental in initiating this support of the PNGV during its early period.

The final report benefited considerably from the insightful comments of the RAND peer reviewers, Robert J. Lempert and John P. White. I am indebted also to David M. Adamson and David Trinkle of RAND for their guidance and help in assembling the mass of material in coherent, literate form.

All errors of fact and judgment are mine. Views expressed here are not necessarily those of RAND or its sponsors.

ACC	Automotive Composites Consortium, a consortium of USCAR
CEO	Chief executive officer
CEQ	Council on Environmental Quality, Office of the President
CIDI	Compression-ignition direct injection (engine)
Clean Car	Early identifier of the goal of PNGV
CRADA	Cooperative research and development agreement
CTI	Critical Technologies Institute
DoC	U.S. Department of Commerce
DoD	U.S. Department of Defense
DoE	U.S. Department of Energy
DoI	U.S. Department of the Interior
EPA	U.S. Environmental Protection Agency
EV-1	All-electric vehicle from General Motors
EWCAP	Electric Wiring Component Application Partnership, a consortium of USCAR
FCCSET	Federal Council for Science, Engineering, and Technology
GM	General Motors
HEV	Hybrid-electric vehicles

Hybrid	Something of mixed origin. In PNGV's case, a combination of two or more technologies
Hybrid-electric	An automotive propulsion system with power provided at any given time either by an electric motor, an engine, or by both in one of several combinations
ICE	Internal combustion engine
LEP/ESST	Low Emissions Partnership/Engine Support Systems Technology, a USCAR consortium
NAS	National Academy of Sciences
NASA	National Aeronautics and Space Administration
NEC	National Economic Council
NIST	National Institute of Standards and Technology
NRC	National Research Council, the research arm of the NAS
NSF	National Science Foundation
OEM	Original equipment manufacturer
OMB	Office of Management and Budget, Office of the President
OSTP	Office of Science and Technology Policy
PEM	Proton exchange membrane (or polymer electrolyte membrane)
PNGV	Partnership for a New Generation of Vehicles. Formed by the U.S. government and the Big Three domestic automobile manufacturers.
R&D	Research and development
RaDiUS	Research and Development in the United States
SAE	Society of Automotive Engineers International
SCAAP	Super Computer Automotive Applications Partnership, a consortium of USCAR
Super car	Sometimes used to refer to the production prototype that is to result from PNGV
SUV	Sport utility vehicle

USABC   United States Advanced Battery Consortium, a consortium of USCAR

USAMP   United States Advanced Materials Partnership, a consortium of USCAR

USCAR   United States Council for Automotive Research, an organization supported by Ford, Chrysler, and General Motors, engaged in collaborative, precompetitive, generic research.   The government's industry partner in PNGV

VRP   Vehicle Recycling Research Partnership, a consortium of USCAR

ZEV   Zero emission vehicle

Chapter One

INTRODUCTION

I have learned this at least by my experiment: if one advances confidently in the direction of his dreams . . . he will meet with a success unexpected in common hours.

—Henry David Thoreau, Walden, *1854*

In *The Machine That Changed the World,* Womack, Jones, and Roos (1990) described the worldwide move from mass production to lean production. In particular, they portrayed the Japanese auto industry as soaring above its competition, with unflattering comparisons to the U.S. "Big Three" domestic automobile manufacturers.

Today, several years after the study that led to the book, the Big Three have drawn abreast of their Japanese competitors by most measures of productivity and profitability. However, the U.S. government perceived that additional gains in Big Three's manufacturing productivity would be necessary to ensure continued industry competitiveness. Other problems, such as the environmental impact of the automobile, were considered important to address as well. As a result, the government and the Big Three have combined in a partnership that, if successful, should result in the industry being a generation ahead in technologies key to automotive design, engineering, and manufacturing.

The Partnership for a New Generation of Vehicles (PNGV) was announced September 29, 1993, by President Bill Clinton in the Rose Garden of the White House. The chief executives of the Big Three domestic automobile manufacturers and the president of the United

Auto Workers were present, as was Vice President Al Gore; Dr. John Gibbons, the President's Science Advisor; and Dr. Mary L. Good, Under Secretary for Technology, Department of Commerce (DoC).

The DoC was designated the lead agency for civilian technology within the government early in the Clinton administration. The PNGV thus fell under the aegis of Dr. Good. To prosecute the working details of the partnership, the PNGV Secretariat was formed, the director of which reported to Dr. Good. The author served in that position from early 1994 until the spring of 1997. What follows is based on the author's involvement in the PNGV from its formative stage through the point where candidate advanced technologies were being selected for concept vehicles and, later, production prototypes of the "new generation of vehicles." To some extent, this represents a self-evaluation of the effectiveness of a particular approach to managing a singular kind of government research and development (R&D) enterprise.

PURPOSE AND SCOPE OF THIS REPORT

This report documents the approach taken to managing the government side of PNGV and what has been learned from its initial, organizing phases. The motivation is to provide guidance to those embarking on similar government-industry partnerships in the future. In so doing, the positive features of PNGV may be emulated, and potential problem areas may be recognized and circumvented.

The term *partnership* has come to be applied to a wide array of types of cooperative arrangements. To provide a meaningful basis for comparison, this report considers PNGV relative only to other cooperative efforts between industry and government that go beyond the traditional models of regulations or federal contracts for research. Furthermore, the focus is on partnerships that foster the development and implementation of new technologies. Consequently, this discussion will not include private-only efforts or service-related partnerships.

It is well to mention what aspects of the PNGV will not be covered in this report. Generally, topics relating to industry's experiences with product development, potential future directions of engineering efforts, the specific amounts of resources individual companies are dedicating to their PNGV projects, and so on, will not be discussed.

Similarly, the implications of business deals, ventures, or partnerships for future PNGV relationships will not be covered here, as they are speculative and best left for industry comment. Finally, this report is not intended to provide a thorough history of the PNGV and does not entail a critical assessment of the success of the partnership. As indicated in the Preface, other sources serve these functions.

The report concentrates on the managerial considerations of the government side of the PNGV. The environment from the inception of the partnerships and the challenges encountered are discussed. There is also a review of the lessons that might be derived from the PNGV experience. This is meant to highlight the issues that could determine the ultimate success or failure of a similar enterprise.

BACKGROUND: GOALS AND VISION OF THE PNGV

Government partnerships are very much in vogue these days; there are partnerships with the private sector and with states, cities, and foreign entities. The government has had many partnerships with industry in the past, for example, with aviation, agriculture, and other industrial enterprises. Government-industry relationships during wartime have many of the characteristics of partnerships.

The PNGV was created under a very special set of circumstances; although government-industry partnerships are not unique, this one has a distinguishing set of characteristics. These include the addressing of a large number of socioeconomic, environmental, and national security issues; involving three very large industrial firms; tapping ongoing R&D projects rather than initiating new funding; and adhering closely to government's position as a source of advanced technology and to industry's role in the marketplace.

The ultimate objective of this partnership is a production prototype of a vehicle that may, in whole or in derivative components, be offered for sale to the public. This may differ from the objectives of future government-industry partnerships. Nevertheless, the approach taken to managing the partnership may be applicable to other, similar collaborative technical enterprises.

Among the goals agreed upon for the partnership was the development of technologies for a vehicle (which came to be known as the "clean car" or "super car") with the following attributes:

- 80 miles per gallon, three times that of today's cars
- Substantially reduced emissions, meeting the Environmental Protection Agency's Tier II standards
- Improved recyclability, to 80 percent of the vehicle from the present 75 percent
- Affordability comparable to that of today's sedans
- Meeting established vehicle safety standards.[1]

Other goals for the PNGV were to "significantly improve national competitiveness in manufacturing," and to "implement commercially viable innovations from ongoing research in conventional vehicles."

The reality of the formidable price-value standard of today's mass-produced cars makes the technical performance goals of the PNGV especially daunting. The industry has accumulated more than 100 years of experience in vehicle design, manufacture, and production. The implicit promise of the PNGV is a higher level of performance, with improved miles per gallon and reduced emissions, while maintaining all other vehicle attributes, including affordability.

This problem has been addressed by assuming that a step increase in the level of technology must be achieved. This is in contrast with traditional conservative engineering, which follows a linear approach to product development. In such a model, incremental improvement is favored over radical leaps into the unknown. However, given the gains desired for the PNGV—a 40-percent weight reduction, a doubling of propulsion efficiency, and so on—conventional materials and components cannot be improved sufficiently regardless of the amount of incremental gains achieved.

The industry executives agreed to have their firms collaborate in an effort that would culminate in an advanced-technology production prototype by 2004.[2] The government agreed to make the resources of its national laboratories available to the automobile industry.

---

[1] For a complete set of goals, see DoC (1995).

[2] The terms of the agreement for the partnership may be found in Executive Office of the President (1993).

Additionally, the government agreed to perform or support research as necessary to achieve the goals of the partnership.

Simply having more-advanced technologies is no guarantee of being competitive—especially when compared with the Japanese auto industry. However, the partnership has been sensitive to that point; there is an agreement to bring the technologies together, first in concept vehicles and later, at the end of the program, in production prototypes.

Presuming the partnership is ultimately successful, the Big Three should enjoy a competitive advantage and be among the first to market with new technology. In that case, they may be referred to as "The Machine that Could revolutionize automobile technology." Through this collaborative effort with the government, the industry thus may be able to maximize its technical strengths to move a generation ahead of its competition. At the same time, it will have addressed important social goals without forcing the government to resort to mandates or regulatory mechanisms.

ORGANIZATION OF THE REPORT

Chapter Two discusses the environment surrounding the inception of the partnership and the initial challenges encountered. Chapter Three attempts to derive lessons from the PNGV experience and highlights issues that could determine the ultimate success or failure of a similar enterprise. Chapter Four presents the author's personal insights on participants' attitudes and preconceptions that influenced aspects of the partnership and in some cases presented initial obstacles that had to be overcome. Chapter Five offers conclusions.

After completion of the first draft, Chapter Six was added to describe recent developments in the PNGV, some of which are occurring earlier than anticipated. These developments signal a higher likelihood of success for the partnership than previously assumed. The reviewers of the first draft strongly urged expanding this report to take the developments into account. The afterword therefore briefly describes the original equipment manufacturers' (OEMs') recently deployed experimental cars, foreign automobile developments, progress in selecting the most promising PNGV technologies, and their significance. Finally, some thoughts have been included on the future direction of the PNGV and what might follow.

Chapter Two

LAUNCHING THE PARTNERSHIP

> I have an enterprise that is without precedent. . . .
>
> —*Jean Jacques Rousseau*, Les Confessions *[1781–1788]*

This chapter describes the PNGV from an organizational standpoint, discussing motivations for the partnership, its uniqueness, the relationships of the participants and the environment in which they are operating, details on management of the government side, and the handling of technical issues. The chapter concludes with an outline of the advantages PNGV possesses and the problems to be faced—not all of which have been surmounted completely.[1]

MOTIVATIONS FOR THE PARTNERSHIP

A number of factors appeared to have converged to precipitate the formation of the PNGV.[2] Within the government, the Federal Council for Science, Engineering, and Technology (FCCSET) was established by statute in 1976. It was chaired by the Director of the

---

[1]David Trinkle of RAND is completing an analysis of the PNGV that addresses these problems more directly. His study examines the partnership as a policy response to a societal problem and explores how it compares with possible alternative approaches and how well it might apply to other industries or technological issues. This study is to be completed in 1998.

[2]The material of this section is drawn primarily from the Harvard University Kennedy School of Government case study of PNGV (Bunten, 1997), supplemented by interviews with individuals in the government preceding the formation of PNGV.

Office of Science and Technology Policy (OSTP), who reports to the President of the United States. In the latter days of the Bush administration, the FCCSET, in turn, formed the Advanced Manufacturing Technology Initiative. Its goal was to accelerate the development of advanced manufacturing technologies to meet national needs.[3] This group consisted of members from most of the technical agencies: the Department of Agriculture, the DoC, the Department of Defense, the Department of Energy (DoE), the Environmental Protection Agency, the Federal Emergency Management Agency, the Department of the Interior, the National Aeronautics and Space Administration (NASA), the National Institutes of Health, and the National Science Foundation (NSF). Its initial focus was on promoting synergy in manufacturing R&D among federal agencies.

At about the same time, there was concern within the national laboratories about potential funding reductions as a consequence of the end of the Cold War. The laboratories believed they had capabilities that might be applied to national technical problems other than weapon systems. The environmental problems ascribed to automobiles were one issue the labs believed they might contribute to solving.

Within the auto industry, batteries emerged as a problem all three companies agreed needed attention. Technical reasons aside, there was also the specter of the zero emission vehicle (ZEV) mandate imposed by California in 1990. It stipulated that 2 percent of the cars sold in 1998 should be ZEVs, with increasing percentages in following years. Practically, ZEV standards could only be met with battery-powered cars.

So mutual interests drew both the government and the Big Three toward improving electrical energy storage. After protracted discussions between government and industry and among the three car companies, the U.S. Advanced Battery Consortium (USABC) was formed in 1991.

The car companies' experience with USABC showed them that they could work together and with the government productively on generic, precompetitive research. Other consortia followed, such as

---

[3]At that time, there was widespread concern about the competitiveness of the United States in key economic sectors, especially in the automobile industry.

the Vehicle Recycling Partnership. By 1992, this activity increased to the point that an overseeing management mechanism was needed, and the U.S. Council for Automotive Research (USCAR) was formed. The form of the PNGV took shape in discussions between the government and USCAR starting in 1992. USCAR was the entity designated to manage the industry research supporting the partnership.

Most of the industry people who participated in USABC helped organize the PNGV at the staff level. The relative ease with which the industry responded to the needs of the partnership was a consequence of their having learned to work with each other and the government under USABC.

During the 1992 presidential campaign, Bill Clinton promised to have the government promote civilian high-tech projects (Clinton and Gore, 1992, pp. 143–145). At the same time, he endorsed the proposal to increase the Corporate Average Fuel Economy standard progressively to 45 miles per gallon by the year 2105.

Once the new Clinton administration was installed, the prior work of FCCSET became known. FCCSET evolved into the National Science and Technology Council, under OSTP. A working group was formed to oversee automotive technology progress within the government. This group outlined in rough form the three goals that later were refined with industry to become the PNGV's goals. At about this time, President Clinton and Vice President Gore became aware of the group's conclusion that a fuel-efficient, environmentally friendly vehicle was possible. Word came down to them that "the President wants to do a clean car." Dr. John Gibbons, the director of OSTP and the President's science advisor, suggested approaching the automobile industry about a partnership to achieve improved automobile fuel efficiency and reduced emissions.

Discussions were initiated with the representatives of the Big Three. It is fair to say that the primary motivation of the industry was to avoid federally mandated fuel efficiency and emissions standards. On the government side, the objective became broader as the talks proceeded: Improved fuel efficiency was seen as a means to reduce dependence on imported oil and therefore to improve the balance of payments in addition to enhancing national security. The prospects for reduced auto emissions also tied in with the many environmentally related initiatives of the administration.

A voluntary government-industry partnership had considerable appeal to the administration in that it avoided a confrontation with the Big Three, which constituted the largest industrial sector in the nation.

The industry on its part saw an opportunity to avoid being portrayed as consistently opposing the safety and environmental improvements the government advocated.

OSTP performed an analysis of what was needed in the way of reductions in greenhouse gases to meet the 1992 Global Warming Treaty signed by President George Bush. The analysis showed that an improvement of three to four times in fuel efficiency was needed. As an alternative, an increase in the federal gas tax was considered to reduce fuel consumption. However, an increase of 25 cents per gallon was believed necessary to produce the necessary effect. This proved not to be feasible politically.

Additionally, the administration believed that the substantial technology resources of the national laboratories held real promise to assist the auto industry. These factors, on both the government and industry sides, converged in the agreement to proceed with PNGV. This agreement was announced by President Clinton September 29, 1993, in the Rose Garden of the White House with industry and government leaders present.

Given the above conditions, the PNGV might have been launched a bit earlier. However, the industry needed the assurance that the technical options were feasible and that it was possible to work productively in partnership with the government. The experience with the relatively successful USABC collaboration reassured both the industry and the government that they could work together. The thought of taking on the very encompassing PNGV was therefore not as daunting as it otherwise might have been.

THE UNIQUENESS AND SIGNIFICANCE OF THE PNGV

The PNGV is not the first partnership between government and industry to develop new technologies. Indeed, even before the beginnings of PNGV, partnerships were already beginning to appear in various shapes and sizes in several industries. Perhaps the best known example is SEMATECH, a partnership created in 1987 among semiconductor manufacturers and the Defense Advanced Research

Projects Agency. Such efforts were made possible with the passage of federal legislation in recent decades that removed antitrust barriers to corporate collaboration in research.[4]   In particular, the 1984 National Cooperative Research Act provided companies with new options for coordinating their research efforts (Coburn, 1995, p. 10).[5]

Likewise, the PNGV is not the first partnership between the government and the U.S. automotive industry. Examples include consortia in composite materials, vehicle recycling, and other programs that, prior to PNGV, involved the individual OEMs of the Big Three with a single federal agency (typically DoE). Perhaps most notable among the formal consortia developed before the PNGV was the 1991 creation of the USABC. Indeed, as is indicated elsewhere in this report, not only did USABC and other consortia predate PNGV, but their very existence facilitated its conception and implementation.

However, several aspects of the PNGV demonstrate its uniqueness among partnerships and, in the larger sense, its significance as a potential model for coordinating R&D efforts across distinct and dissimilar organizations. The purpose of this section is to consider the uniqueness and significance of the PNGV among the other government-industry technology partnerships. It begins with a definition of partnerships and outlines many existing types of partnerships. The rest of the section discusses the specific characteristics of the PNGV that distinguish it from other partnerships and that provide a preliminary basis for determining how PNGV lessons might be applied to other partnerships, both existing and future.[6]

What Characterizes a Partnership?

The term *partnership* is used to designate a wide range of cooperative efforts that vary dramatically in structure, funding, purpose, and many other dimensions. The term itself only indicates that the effort

---

[4]By some definitions of *partnership*, one could note certain efforts in agriculture or defense before this time. However, as indicated in the introduction, we review the PNGV in the context of a tighter definition of the term.

[5]This section was written by David Trinkle, as adapted from a draft of his doctoral dissertation assessing the PNGV.

[6]Application of these lessons is further considered elsewhere in this report and in David Trinkle's forthcoming dissertation.

has some sort of cooperative component, as opposed to more straightforward mechanisms involving the transfer of funds for services, such as contracts or grants. Some dimensions of typical partnerships, as drawn from a historical survey of partnership efforts, are outlined in Table 1. As indicated in the table, partnerships may be defined by several dimensions having to do with the purpose of the

Table 1

Dimensions of a Partnership

Attributes	Components
Purpose of the partnership	Overall motivations
Nature of the industry	Type, size, structure, location, maturity Distribution of funding and other resources Global nature, relative U.S. competitiveness History of federal interaction Political factors Industry associations and other players
Organization of the partnership	
Goals	Types, revolutionary nature Nature of goals Underlying motivations for goals Motivations of participants
Membership and structure	Types of members, exclusivity of membership Horizontal and vertical components of collaboration Dues or other barriers to participation Cultural factors Rigidity/flexibility of structure
Funding and legal mechanisms	Level of total funding Level and nature of federal contribution Level and nature of industry contribution
Working arrangements	Management structure and style Technical organization Facilities Intellectual property
Accountability	Requirements, metrics, formal review
Life cycle	Term Commitment Renewal Exit strategy

partnership, the nature of the industry, and various factors of the way the partnership is organized.

Even within the limited scope of the partnerships considered in this report, government-industry technology partnerships can vary tremendously. They may include a number of organizations and legal mechanism, such as cooperative research and development agreements (CRADAs), consortia, and cofunded contracts. They can be international or strictly domestic. The federal component can consist of access to federal research or the provision of federal funding to industry for research. Indeed, any and all of the dimensions indicated in Table 1 can vary from one partnership to the next.

What Makes PNGV Unique?

While Table 1 illustrates the many characteristics that can define a partnership, the PNGV stands out in five fundamental areas:

- the nature of the automotive industry
- its history
- the goals of the partnership
- the structure of the partnership
- the funding of the partnership.

While the nature and history of the automotive industry suggest that the setting for the partnership was unique, the characteristics of the PNGV itself demonstrate how a partnership can coordinate the efforts of distinct organizations, overcoming and capitalizing upon such features of its industry. Furthermore, the industry setting and the resulting policy response also provide a preliminary basis for determining how PNGV lessons might be applied to other existing and future partnerships. The rest of this section discusses the PNGV in these five areas.

The Nature of the Industry. The nature of the domestic automotive industry is significant in three primary areas: size, market concentration, and geographical concentration.

The automotive industry is among the largest industrial sectors in the United States. In 1996, the Big Three spent $17.3 billion on research and development.[7] By comparison, this exceeds the 1996 R&D expenditures of NASA, the DOE, and the National Science Foundation (NSF) combined.[8] General Motors, Ford, and Chrysler are the first, second, and fourth in exports among U.S. companies. It should not be surprising that the automotive industry is considered to be vital to the country's commerce.

With regard to structure, the Big Three together constitute a large share of the world automotive market. Within the United States, the Big Three account for virtually all of the automotive manufacturing capability.

Geographically, most of the divisions and plants of the domestic automakers and their suppliers are clustered within the Midwest, not far from Detroit. Indeed, the lack of this sort of geographical proximity among the auto manufacturers in the European Union is likely to provide a barrier to its analogous effort (in addition, of course, to issues of culture, language, historical biases, etc.).

Thus, the domestic automotive industry stands out in its significance within the nation's economy (and that of the world). A partnership that includes these giants of industry is unique, if for no other reason. While the proximity of manufacturers is not unheard of in other industries, this proximity is an advantage the Big Three have over analogous foreign efforts.

The History of the Industry. The history of the automotive industry in the United States is significant in three respects. First, from a technology standpoint, the automotive industry can be characterized as having a century of experience with automobiles based on the internal combustion engine, its power train, and other characteristics of present-day vehicles. This familiarity means that, slowly and incrementally during these 100 years, performance has been optimized; manufacturing techniques have minimized costs; and the manufacturing, marketing, fueling, and other aspects of the infra-

---

[7]Except where noted, the statistics in this paragraph are from the American Automobile Manufacturers Association (URL: **http://www.aama.com**).

[8]In FY96, NASA, DOE, and NSF spent, respectively, $9.1 billion, $5.5 billion, and $2.2 billion on R&D. Together, these agencies spent $16.8 billion of the $69.6 billion spent on R&D (not including facilities) by the Federal government in FY96. These and other statistics on government spending were taken from RAND's RaDiUS© database on federally funded R&D, as derived from multiple government data systems.

structure behind the industry have been geared to work with internal combustion engines. Thus, not only do the existing technologies have the advantage of being proven over time, but there is also a major infrastructure developed to support these specific technologies.

Consequently, the introduction of new technologies into the automotive industry faces potentially tremendous barriers because of the maturity of the industry and the associated infrastructure. The revolutionary improvements in cost and performance required to achieve the PNGV goals (as discussed later in this report) are thus remarkable for the challenge they represent.

The second issue of historical significance is the nature of the relationship between the automakers and the state and federal governments over time. This could best be characterized as frequently antagonistic. For example, safety and emissions standards have been established at various times through the use of federal or state mandates or other legislative mechanisms. The model for this interaction was that the automakers would generally resist new, untried technologies unless the government forced them to change.

Thus, a partnership in which the goals and approaches have been negotiated voluntarily with the industry instead of mandated is also remarkable. Giving industry the technical lead in meeting these negotiated goals truly breaks the mold of the traditional antagonistic, legislating-and-mandating relationship.

A third significant issue is the heterogeneity among the OEMs with respect to their experience interacting with the government on R&D through contracts. Specifically, while General Motors and Ford were experienced with government R&D contracts, Chrysler was not. As a result, General Motors and Ford were much more used to interacting with the government and were faster to move in conjunction with government efforts. For example, Chrysler had initially declined to participate in the DoE's hybrid vehicle program (which would later become part of the PNGV). Chrysler later joined this and other cooperative efforts, but the hesitation is thought to have been due in large part to the company's lack of familiarity at that time with government R&D contracts.[9]

---

[9]Personal observation by the author of this report.

The Goals of the Partnership. The multiple factors motivating the PNGV tie into many of the nation's priorities. Such motivations as competitiveness, energy security, the environment, and balance of trade, however, are not necessarily consistent in the policy solutions they might suggest independently. These seemingly unrelated goals make the partnership a unique, complex effort. More specifically, the explicit statement of international competitiveness as the goal for the partnership is a new feature among federal efforts in the automotive industry (U.S. Congress, 1995, p. 231).

In fact, the PNGV goals arose from the factors motivating not just the federal government but other stakeholders as well. The goals were negotiated between the government and industry to capture the many priorities of the federal government, its agencies, the general public, and the domestic automotive industry.

Furthermore, the goals are ambitious. For example, the stated goal for production prototypes of passenger vehicles with fuel efficiencies of 80 miles per gallon is not trivial. The fact that existing materials and technologies used in contemporary vehicles cannot achieve that level of efficiency forces the participants to look at revolutionary new technologies.

The Structure of the Partnership. The uniqueness of the structure of the PNGV is found in its membership and in the way the research is conducted and managed.

With respect to membership, PNGV was designed to include the coordinated efforts of several federal agencies with the OEMs. The involvement of multiple agencies is significant in itself; where other federal R&D efforts in automotive technologies have suffered from agency parochialism, PNGV has allowed greater interagency coordination (U.S. Congress, 1995, p. 229). Similarly, the industry side comprises multiple partners, principally the Big Three domestic OEMs. The structure of the partnership thus has a horizontal component in both government and industry membership.

In addition, there is also a vertical component to the partnership. On the industry side, the supply chain of the OEMs is considered to be an integral part of the partnership. To varying degrees among the individual OEMs, the suppliers often do a large share of the R&D for specific technical components. In a manner of speaking, there is also a vertical component on the federal side of the partnership, through the contribution of colleges and universities to agency-funded research.

However, with its goal of U.S. industrial competitiveness, the partnership was designed to focus on domestic manufacturers, a criterion that implicitly excluded the majority of foreign OEMs.[10] At the same time, the Big Three have been left to include their suppliers, as appropriate. In some instances, these suppliers include foreign manufacturers.

While the partnership is managed by steering groups and coordinating committees consisting of both government and industry representatives, the technical lead was left to the industry. Thus, while the overall goals were conceived by the government and negotiated between government and industry, the most appropriate technological solutions to achieve those goals were left to the industry to select. Thus, by not dictating solutions, the government allows the industry to arrive at the technologies that are most effective with respect to performance, cost, and market acceptance.

In the same spirit, the management of the partnership has a relatively flexible structure. While some have criticized this as a weakness, this flexibility allows the partnership to grow and adapt as technologies are investigated and the partnership matures.

Funding of the Partnership. The PNGV was designed to take advantage of existing research within the government. The program's "budget" is a virtual one; overall expenditures are a total of amounts from otherwise unrelated efforts in distinct agencies.[11] Thus, while the federal funding for the PNGV has at times been estimated at about $300 million, this figure is determined from the combination of independent efforts and does not exist as a unified budget. In contrast, SEMATECH, for example, included transfers of federal funds of more than $100 million per year as specific contributions to the industrial collaboration. The ramifications of the PNGV's lack of a central budget are discussed later in this report.

---

[10]Of course, distinctions between "domestic" and "foreign" manufacturers are increasingly difficult to make, with the trend toward multinational firms, especially in the automotive industry.

[11]As discussed in the "Management Approach" section of this report.

Comparing a $300 million annual funding level with other efforts makes it seem relatively high, although between the rough estimation of the federal funding and the notional, unverified matching of industry funds, it is difficult to compare this to the funding for other efforts.

INITIAL ORGANIZATION

Much of the organization, the relationships between participants, and the operating procedures were developed as PNGV evolved. Others have documented those aspects, but briefly stated, the activity of the first few months, October 1993 through spring 1994, may be described as devoted to getting organized and learning how to work together.[12] This principally involved senior management people who later became the Operational Steering Group, the guidance and policy body for the partnership. They formulated the organizational structure of the groups reporting to it. The management structure they developed is shown in Figure 1.

The next phase, through mid-1995, engaged the Technical Task Force in developing plans and translating them into action documents for technical teams. From then through late 1996, candidate technologies were examined, evaluated relative to PNGV goals, and tested analytically in notional vehicle applications. From a management standpoint, the center of activity was the group formed on the industry side: the Technical Planning Managers. This group, known as TRIAD, works directly with the technical teams that report to them. On the government side, the TRIAD is supported by the Technical Council, which contains technical specialists selected from some of the participating agencies. As of the Technology Selection phase in 1997, this process has culminated in a selection of the technologies considered to show the most promise for meeting the goals of the program.

While technology evaluations and selections were in progress, the individual auto companies surfaced preliminary concept cars that incorporated a substantial amount of PNGV's technological thinking.

---

[12]See Bunten (1997) and Hillebrand (1996).

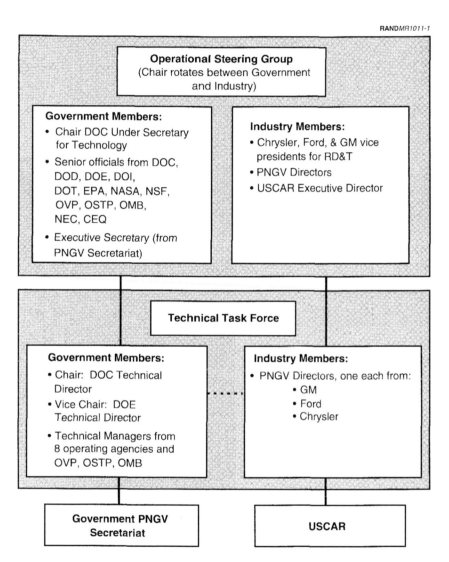

SOURCE: DoC (1995), p. 2-1.

Figure 1—Initial PNGV Management Structure

These included the hybrid-electric Intrepid ESX Chrysler introduced at the 1996 Detroit Auto Show and the fuel cell power train the company presented at the 1997 Detroit Auto Show. Ford displayed its advanced technology Synergy 2010 in the fall of 1995 and recently revealed the details of its P2000 research vehicle. General Motors launched the EV-1, an all-electric vehicle that incorporated considerable PNGV technology, in the spring of 1996.[13]

A summary of the technical accomplishments to that time was published in the summer of 1996 (USCAR, 1996). The report contains 65 accomplishments and their significance relative to PNGV goals, described in detail along with the principal contributors.

The early graphical representation of the partnership showed two interconnected rings, one for government, one for industry. As the thinking evolved, it was recognized that technology was the focus of the partnership and that, in the main, technology resided with the suppliers, universities, and others from the technical community of the OEMs (Chrysler, Ford, and General Motors). As a consequence, the relationship is now portrayed as having three rings, as depicted in Figure 2. The "others" refers to individual inventors, small business, and nontraditional sources of potentially useful automobile technology, commonly referred to on the government side of the partnership as the "creative track." The dashed line in Figure 2 is meant to indicate the nonexplicit inclusion of this third group, whereas the solid line denotes the formal PNGV partnership.

TECHNICAL ORGANIZATION

Technical teams are the core of the partnership's activities. They provide the means by which candidate technologies are explored and considered for vehicle application. The PNGV organizational structure as of early 1997 is shown in Figure 3. All the technical teams and the management positions are staffed with both government and industry people.   For reasons explained in the "Management Approach" section, industry assumed the leadership of the technical teams. The cross-matrix nature of the organization

---

[13]More recent developments are covered in the Afterword, Chapter Six.

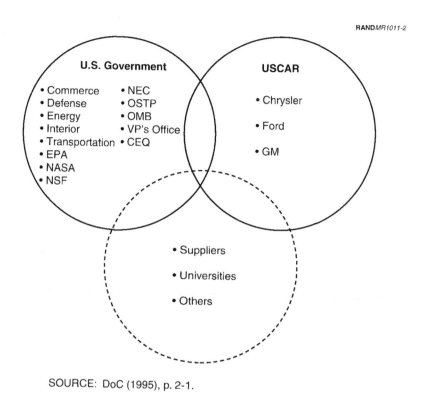

RAND*MR1011-2*

SOURCE: DoC (1995), p. 2-1.

Figure 2—PNGV Participants' Relationship

structure may be seen, as well as the supporting position of the several consortia.[14] The hierarchical structure shows the progression from technical specialization, to oversight, to management, and ultimately to policy guidance by the government-industry Operational Steering Group.

Whereas the positions immediately above the technical teams are staffed with full-time managers, the members of the teams are part-timers. This is a significant consideration: The team members have

---

[14]The abbreviations for the consortia are provided in the Glossary.

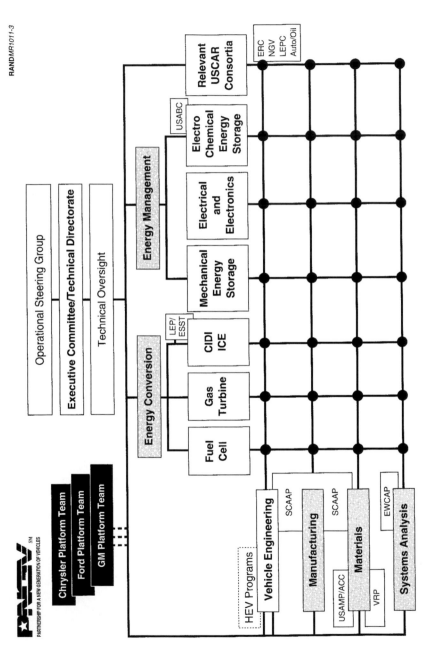

Figure 3—PNGV Technical Organizational Structure

other jobs that demand at least one-half of their time. Some technical teams meet about once a month; most meet more often. Many meet every other week, some weekly. The government lab representatives are fully immersed in the problem solving, on an equal basis with their industry partners. The issues the teams address range from esoteric research details to practical questions relating to the application of technology to real-world problems.

The cross-matrix structure brings technical specialists in materials and manufacturing in contact with each component technology. Such issues as materials cost and formability are thus addressed by experts. The Systems Analysis Technical Team assesses the potential of each candidate technology to meet the performance goals for the vehicles. Finally, the Vehicle Engineering Technical Team evaluates the practical compatibility of the many components under consideration and how they might fit and function in experimental vehicles.

While all this activity proceeds, the engineers in each company's platform teams evaluate technology developments. These will be incorporated into their experimental vehicles and, later, into their versions of the ultimate PNGV production prototypes.

The Executive Committee oversees all this technical activity. Its members, who serve full time, are the chairman and vice chairman of the government's technical task force and the three PNGV directors, one from each of the automobile companies.

The Operational Steering Group provides policy guidance to the Executive Committee. This body contains government and industry officials. On the government side, the chairperson is the Under Secretary for Technology of the DoC, the lead agency for the partnership. The other government members from the participating agencies are of roughly similar rank. On the industry side, the chair rotates among the senior vice presidents for research or technology at the OEMs. As noted in Figure 1, the chair for Operational Steering Group meetings alternates from government to industry.

Figure 4 illustrates a more encompassing representation of the PNGV organization that David Trinkle has developed as part of a doctoral dissertation for the RAND Graduate School (Trinkle, forthcoming). This figure shows various stakeholders involved in the PNGV process, both the participants actively involved in the partnership and the other stakeholders playing some external role, such as observing or monitoring. The oval marked "PNGV" is meant to delineate this distinction: Within it are the organizations that interact as active participants. The lines between them represent their primary interactions; the heavier lines indicate more significant relationships in the con-

RAND*MR1011-4*

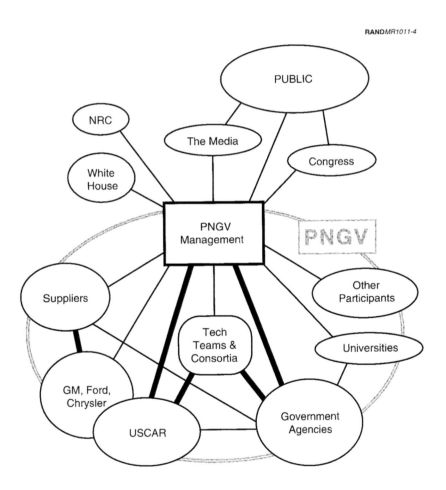

Figure 4—The PNGV Extended Community

text of the PNGV.[15] Thus, the PNGV management coordinates with the federal agencies and the USCAR consortia, which all work together through the PNGV technical teams. The industry side shows the role of the suppliers, which interact in the partnership primarily through the strong bonds with the Big Three and USCAR.

The organizations outside the "PNGV" oval include the executive and legislative bodies that steer or oversee the partnership; the National Research Council (NRC), which provides formal periodic reviews; the Media, which publicize or comment on the progress of the effort; and, finally, the general public. Indeed, the individuals that constitute this body form a significant stakeholder group through their roles as taxpayers; consumers; and, ultimately, beneficiaries of the results of the effort.

In addition to what is shown in the figure, the extended community also includes other nonparticipants—organizations that interact with the auto industry that are *not* well-represented in PNGV. These include foreign auto companies; small, independent domestic manufacturers; and industries indirectly related to automobiles or manufacturing, all of which may be interested in this major effort.

INITIAL ENVIRONMENT

The media's initial reaction to the announcement of the PNGV ranged from disapproval to a mild skepticism that anything useful could come from "big government" and the "Big Three" working together. Within a week of the announcement, a cartoon appeared (Figure 5) lampooning the car project. Others followed that suggested, crudely in one case, that the taxpayer was to be a victim of the partnership (Figure 6). With time, as the approach being taken became known more widely, the media responded more favorably.

The NRC's first peer review committee recognized the need for a public-relations effort. Their report stressed the importance of out-

---

[15]Of course, there are many other interactions than those shown in the figure, and the components and their relationships are somewhat dependent on the context in which they are discussed.

Figure 5—Early Editorial Comment

Figure 6—Creative Portrayal of the Partnership

reach to interested groups, especially the environmentalists. Unstated, but generally understood, was the need to overcome the poor image the Big Three had with such groups (NRC, 1994).

The government side of the partnership was structured, in the main, to tap into existing research resources and ongoing projects. Aside from allowing a faster start, this approach defused criticism that PNGV was another big government "tax and spend" program.[16]

The 1994 congressional election, held about a year after the onset of the PNGV, resulted in a shift of the majority of both houses to the Republican, opposition, party. As a Democratic administration initiative, the PNGV drew immediate criticism from the new Congress. This was part of a widespread hostility to programs considered "corporate welfare" or embodying "industrial policy."

To counter criticism—or to anticipate it, in most cases—we contacted and briefed key congressional staffers on committees having oversight of programs related to the PNGV in participating agencies. The staffers responded most positively to industry briefers—because of their "car talk." This was a bit of an ego problem for the government managers, but the pragmatic conclusion was, "Go with what works!"

Reporters for the automotive trade press, although initially skeptical, were nonetheless curious about how the very ambitious goals of the PNGV could possibly be achieved. Technical briefings at national labs, "show and tell" sessions, were arranged for them. After seeing tangible developments directed at solving specific problems, the reporters without exception appeared favorably impressed. As an understanding of the PNGV grew—within the automotive trade press, in particular—its public image improved. Today, with the exception of some special-interest advocacy groups, the PNGV appears to be viewed quite favorably by the public. The mechanics of turning around this negative public environment will not be dealt with here. Rather, the significant aspects of the program that convinced reasonable people to become supportive are described in the following sections.

---

[16]See discussion in "Management Approach" section.

MANAGEMENT APPROACH

A number of the features of the partnership's management are mentioned elsewhere. They represent a means for managing the government side of a government-industry cooperative R&D effort that, in total, had not been tried before. The major points are as follows.

Partnership Within the Government

In addition to the partnership with industry, a partnership was established within the government. The relationship between the Big Three domestic automobile producing firms and the federal government is the widely recognized basis for the PNGV. The partnership of the seven participating agencies and their 19 laboratories is less appreciated.[17] There is no internal directive compelling these governmental units to support the program. Their involvement has been a consequence of mutual interest and a desire to support administration initiatives. A third component of the partnership includes the supplier, university, and individual inventor communities. The suppliers may be further categorized as either traditional—having an established relationship with the OEMs—or nontraditional. The latter are principally aerospace and defense firms with advanced technology they believe has utility for automobiles. Again, these relationships are shown in Figure 2.

Budgetary Arrangement

The partnership operates within existing funding mechanisms without a central budget. Initially, this was dictated by the need to move quickly to establish the program. PNGV was announced two days before the beginning of the next government fiscal year, FY94. In reality, there could be no influence on that budget. Even FY95, which would start a year later, was essentially "locked in": By September 1993, the FY95 budget request had moved from the agencies to the Office of Management and Budget. Although some funds within the DoE were shifted to support PNGV research, the establishment of PNGV had a minimal effect overall on the President's FY95 budget. Therefore, the FY96 budget submission was

---

[17]The Department of the Interior unit initially participating in PNGV was later disestablished, and its functions were transferred to the DoE.

the first opportunity to organize all the R&D activities within the government in support of the partnership. The budgets drawn upon, nevertheless, were those contained within the individual federal agencies. In consideration of the many constraints, this was the most that could be accomplished. No central budget was ever requested for PNGV, and none is planned at this point.

A question frequently asked by those interested in the PNGV was, "What is your budget?" This proved difficult to answer because of the lack of a central budget. Also, a significant number of the projects considered to be supporting PNGV are primarily directed at solving some agency's mission-related problem. Rather than be evasive or resort to circumlocution, I have offered the following: The total of all research activity (from 1994 through 1997) within the government related to or supporting the PNGV is roughly—very roughly—$300 million per year.[18] At this "run" rate, roughly one-third goes to the national laboratories to conduct research and work with the industry. Another third is awarded to suppliers in response to proposals to address specific PNGV technical issues. In addition to traditional automotive industry suppliers, this group includes nontraditional, mostly aerospace industry, suppliers and universities, plus individual inventors and small businesses aspiring to do business in the automotive industry.

The remaining one-third of government funding, again very roughly, goes to the individual OEMs: Chrysler, Ford, and General Motors. This is primarily to support development of hybrid–fuel cell, electric, or advanced engine-powered-vehicle development and evaluation. Roughly three-quarters of the government funds the OEMs receive go through them to the suppliers supporting their new developments.

Suppliers, traditional and nontraditional, therefore receive roughly one-half of the government funding for the PNGV. Most of this flows directly from contracts with the government, but a significant amount of the government's funds for them come via the OEMs.

---

[18]This figure was arrived at via figures compiled by the Office of Management and Budget. Normally, the office's budget figures are absolute and not subjective. In this case, however, judgments had to be made about the proportion of individual research projects that pertained to the PNGV where their primary objective was something other than automotive technology.

As to the scale of the partnership from a funding standpoint, $300 million per year would support a very substantial project in one of the smaller federal agencies, such as the Environmental Protection Agency or NSF. In one of the larger organizations, such as the departments of Defense or Energy, a project of this size would be considered significant, but not among their largest.

The ten-year duration of the PNGV is on the outer reaches for R&D projects. Very few R&D projects are programmed to last that long; when they extend into the ten-year range, they usually are threatened with cancellation.

On the industry side, R&D projects can range from mundane, near-term problem solving with modest budgets to massive efforts leading to product launches. In the latter case, budgets of several billion dollars are not uncommon.

The significance of the PNGV most likely will not turn on the amount of government money spent. Most of this would have been spent anyway on similar, but unfocused, projects. Similarly, the scope of the project probably does not match, at least at present, some of the automakers' product development and introductions. We will have to know the extent to which the industry's next generation of vehicles is more fuel efficient and environmentally friendly yet affordable to consumers before passing final judgment on the partnership's significance.

Utilizing Ongoing Projects

Related government research activities were subsumed to capitalize on existing resources. In addition to the obvious advantage of utilizing ongoing groups or projects, there was also a subtle reason for this approach: the concern that there was a perception that President Clinton's Democratic administration was embarking on a big new "tax and spend" program. A pragmatic approach evolved that sought to make a virtue out of this stark reality:

- The Transportation Energy Efficiency program within DoE was designated as the "core" PNGV technology effort. A project to improve fuel efficiency by two times that had been under way since 1992 was categorized as PNGV.

- Projects in seven other federal agencies that appeared to be relevant were included in PNGV.[19]

- A comprehensive inventory of all ongoing R&D projects within the government considered pertinent to PNGV was prepared and forwarded to USCAR.

- To counter charges of "corporate welfare" emanating from Congress, the point was made that no "new" money had been requested for PNGV; ongoing R&D projects were being tapped or redirected and coordinated.

Industry Assumed Technical Leadership

Industry's assumption of technical leadership recognized that the characteristics of the end product of the partnership, the production prototype, would be driven by market considerations. Technical leadership by industry also avoided any inference that the government was dictating what kind of car would be offered to the American public (caustically referred to as "picking winners and losers").

Government people, especially laboratory scientists, have been fully immersed in the technical proceedings.[20] An early example was the development of a set of operational parameters, e.g., 0 to 60 mph in 12 seconds or less, that defined the targeted performance of the production prototype. These were formulated by the industry and accepted with minor modifications by the government.

Setting Priorities

The initial technical effort was dedicated to determining high-payoff areas for research. Figure 7 was developed in that process. It is from the Program Plan and indicates where the greatest losses in efficiency of a typical automobile may be found. The approach taken is

---

[19]The Department of the Interior unit initially participating in PNGV was later disestablished and its functions transferred to the DoE.

[20]The technical organizational structure (late 1996) is shown in Figure 3.

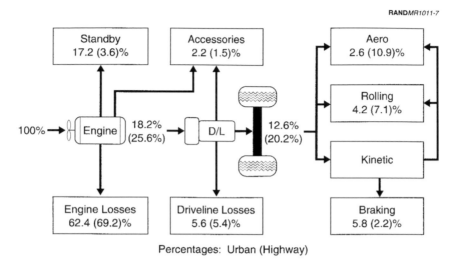

RAND*MR1011-7*

Percentages: Urban (Highway)

SOURCE: DoC (1995), p. 2-1.

Figure 7—Energy Distribution in a Midsize Vehicle

to assume a full supply of energy (e.g., in the gas tank in the case of an internal combustion engine) and examine how it is dissipated through the power train. The losses are shown in the figure as numbers in the boxes; the first relates to energy lost under an urban driving cycle and the second to energy lost under a highway driving cycle. The engine and its accessories may thus be seen as the major consumers of energy, 81.8 percent, under urban driving conditions. Energy is lost there to internal friction and accessories, such as power steering and air conditioning. So the number one priority for research was assigned to engine improvements or alternatives.

The analysis of energy losses proceeds further through the driveline (where another 5.6 percent is lost) to the wheels. It may be seen that only 12.6 percent of the energy in the gas tank is actually applied "where the rubber meets the road." This energy must work against the aerodynamic resistance of the vehicle (which consumes 2.6 percent of original energy) and rolling friction (another 4.2 percent lost) to propel it. The balance of the energy (5.8 percent) is consumed finally when it is converted to heat as the brakes are applied. The magnitude of the energy losses for which these components were responsible determined the amount of attention they received in the PNGV research program.

Technology Competitions

To bring order to the setting of priorities, the candidate projects then were grouped under one of seven technology areas: energy conversion, energy storage, materials, manufacturing, systems analysis, systems engineering, and a general "all else" category. Within each area, the technologies were set in competition with each other in an environment that was referred to as "parallel competitive technology pathways." In the energy conversion area, for example, fuel cells were placed in competition with gas turbines and with advanced piston engines; in energy storage, chemical batteries were in competition with flywheels and with ultracapacitors; and so on. Within a given technology, there was also competition, so that, as another example, proton exchange membrane (PEM) fuel cells were in competition with phosphoric acid fuel cells and with monolithic solid-oxide fuel cells.

Most of the candidate technologies were being funded by government contracts—but not all. One of the most spirited competitions is between steel and aluminum in the materials area. Both industries are engaged in extensive research on means to "lightweight" automobiles to meet PNGV goals (40-percent weight reduction, improved recyclability). No government PNGV funding has flowed to the steel industry. However, in this case, as in several others, competitive advantage has proven a stronger force than the desire for government funding.

Technology Transfer

The popular image of the transfer of technology from a laboratory to a production line is one of an original discovery followed by a unique application. Very few, if any, examples exist of a device invented in a lab being utilized, as is, in a production line. In the case of the PNGV, the government lab projects considered for automotive application were all being pursued originally for other purposes. A new tool, the Research and Development in the United States (RaDiUS) R&D data system,[21] was used to apprise industry engineers of lab activity in areas believed to be of interest. The industry personnel then enlightened the lab scientists about the conditions under which the device (or process) might be adapted for automobile production. This broadened the industry personnel's perspective on the range of new technology that might be applied to a problem. At the same time, the laboratory personnel were exposed to real-world manufacturing considerations; they thus narrowed their field of inquiry. The most productive transfer of technology ensued from this joint, collaborative approach.[22]

Two examples, intelligent induction hardening and fuel cells, will illustrate how technology transfer was effected in the PNGV environment. The hardening technique was developed by Sandia National Laboratory. Sandia's scientists applied knowledge and experience developed from computational modeling and materials characterization studies of how to improve certain weapons. A neural network controller had been developed to control precisely the depth and quality of case-hardened surfaces on steel components that are exposed to high wear. The PNGV materials technical team visited the lab and were briefed on the technique. The potential for stronger, lighter automobile components that could be manufactured with less energy consumption was perceived immediately. However, much discussion ensued between the lab scientists and industry engineers before experimentation led to a practical method for high-rate automobile production. At present, General Motors' Delphi Saginaw Steering Systems is employing the technique to produce intermediate shafts. These are case hardened with a precision five times greater than prior processes and are being incorporated in General Motors Saturn vehicles.

Fuel cells were used as an energy conversion device on NASA's Apollo project, which landed men on the moon in 1969. These were alkali fuel cells, which required pure oxygen and hydrogen for fuel and were not considered practical for family sedans. Early experi-

---

[21]RaDiUS is a data system that contains information on all federally supported R&D. It was developed by RAND to support the Critical Technologies Institute (which in July 1998 was renamed the Science and Technology Policy Institute) and OSTP.

[22]As a consequence, the technology transfer practiced here has often been termed a "contact sport."

ments in applying fuel cells to vehicles involved installing a phosphoric acid fuel cell in a passenger-carrying bus. Although this type of fuel cell functioned reliably, several obstacles were evident when it was considered for automobile propulsion. These included the size and weight of the device, as well as its elevated operating temperature.

Subsequently, the more favorable characteristics of the PEM fuel cell became known. These devices operated at lower temperature and therefore were thought to be potentially more amenable to automobile use from the standpoints of size and weight. The major concern with the PEM fuel cell was its cost: The first estimates were that one produced for automobiles would cost about $30,000. This was principally a consequence of the amount of platinum in the cell, which accounted for more than 80 percent of the cost.

The DoE, which is responsible for developing fuel cells for transportation applications, accelerated PEM development in the national laboratories. As a result, the Los Alamos National Laboratory scientists found a way to apply the catalyst to the polymer membrane using only about 3 percent of the platinum used previously. Scientists at Argonne National Laboratory developed a partial oxidation reformer that operates at ambient pressure. This obviates the need for a compressor—a power-consuming component. Also, the fuel processor is able to operate at a temperature several hundred degrees lower, which means that much less time is needed for startup. At Pacific National Laboratory, a microchannel vaporizer has been developed that allows gasoline to be reformed more readily onboard a vehicle. This also would yield a quicker startup time.

These developments are being incorporated in the PEM fuel cells, which now are estimated to cost at least one-tenth what was originally projected. They will power cars under development by Chrysler, Ford, and General Motors. Each company is following a somewhat different approach, thus allowing several techniques to be evaluated. For example, Chrysler intends to reform gasoline to hydrogen onboard the vehicle. Ford will employ hydrogen stored in pressure vessels, and General Motors, among several of their approaches, will reform methanol onboard to produce the hydrogen needed to feed the fuel cell.

Technology Selection

As the prospects of each candidate technology were evaluated, several things became apparent. Some projects showed real promise of meeting PNGV goal; others may have had tremendous potential but were unlikely to reach fruition within the time frame of the program; and others realistically had poor prospects of meeting any or all of the technical, schedule, or affordability goals.

To allow focusing government resources on the most promising technologies, a "Technology Selection" process was instituted.[23] Its objective was to sort out and prioritize all candidate technologies by the end of calendar year 1997. There has been considerable discussion about the fate of promising projects that, from a timing standpoint, cannot be incorporated into the PNGV production prototype. The general view is that a rationale must be articulated to ensure that R&D in such categories continues beyond the PNGV period.

Documentation and Communications

Priority was given to facilitating communications within the partnership and to keeping interested outside parties informed. This effort took several forms. The first was the *PNGV Program Plan* issued in the summer of 1994 and revised in late 1995 (DoC, 1995). The plan presented the goals of the PNGV research program, milestones, roles of the participants, and resources.

To guide small firms, universities, and individual inventors, *Inventions Needed for PNGV* was published (DoC, 1996). This document identified problem areas in need of solutions. It also indicated which federal agencies were likely to support such research. The intellectual property considerations under government contracts were also explained.

Additionally, an Internet home page was established that contained information on the partnership such as source documents ("Declaration of Intent," etc.), *Program Plan*, and *Inventions Needed*. In addition, the home page lists solicitations from agencies for research related to PNGV.

---

[23]This process was completed on schedule, and the results are reported in DoC-USCAR (1998).

Beyond these mechanisms, government officials involved in PNGV gave numerous presentations at technical symposia, professional society meetings, and other public forums. Numerous magazine and newspaper articles resulted from interviews with key people. There were several television spot stories on PNGV as well. All these communication activities strove to inform the public and maintain an open line of communications into the PNGV program.

Peer Review

The "Declaration of Intent" stipulates that there "be a peer review of PNGV by a disinterested third party, such as the National Academy of Sciences (NAS)."[24] NRC, the operating arm of the National Academy of Sciences, has conducted and issued reports on four peer reviews (NRC, 1994, 1996, 1997, and 1998).

The use of peer reviews to evaluate research proposals is widespread within the government. However, as practiced by the PNGV, the peer review is more of an annual technical board of directors' assessment. A number of the peers, including the chairman, have served on all the reviews from their inception. As a result, they have developed a deep technical knowledge and have provided continuity to the management of the partnership. In addition to oversight of general progress, the peers focus on areas considered key to achieving the program's goals. The 1996 review, for example, concentrated on seven technology areas. Site visits permitted the peers to engage in direct conversations with the researchers in their laboratories. The result of this approach has been incisive reports of great value for the technical direction of the program. Additionally, interested parties, such as Congress, the media, and public interest groups, are given an unbiased appraisal of the partnership's technical progress and prospects for success.

PNGV'S ADVANTAGES

The partnership has had a considerable number of advantages that provided a strong initial momentum:

---

[24]The National Academy of Sciences, founded in 1863 at the request of President Abraham Lincoln, is chartered to "provide advice upon request to the government." It is generally regarded as impartial and eminently qualified in all technical disciplines.

Clear, Easily Understood Goals

"Affordable family sedan," "80 miles per gallon," "reduced emissions," and so on, are all terms the American public can identify with. Everyone seems to be a car expert to some extent; for example, the vast majority of drivers fill their own gas tanks and are sensitive to the price of gasoline. They therefore appreciate the significance of a threefold improvement in fuel efficiency.

Strong Support and Leadership at the Highest Levels of the Administration

President Clinton considers the "Clean Car" to be his initiative; Vice President Gore maintains an active involvement in PNGV; and the president's science advisor, Dr. Gibbons, monitors progress closely. As is always the case when a program has such high-level support, the program manager enjoys a cooperative environment within the organization.

Substantial Depth of Technical Resources Within Federal Laboratories

Twenty federal laboratories are participating in the program. With the exception of the NSF, which has no laboratories, each of the agencies participating in the PNGV has at least one laboratory engaged. Given the diversity of missions of the agencies, military, space, transportation, energy, environmental, etc., there is a tremendous range of technologies to draw upon. Although very few projects were an immediate fit to automotive applications, almost all the technologies considered seriously made a significant contribution.

Diverse Funding Sources

The lack of a central budget was (and continues to be) considered a disadvantage. Funds supporting PNGV R&D are dispersed through 12 separate funding sources, six from each of the House and Senate appropriations bills. However, depending on the political climate, the lack of a central budget can also be an advantage. Because of its multiple funding sources, the budget for the partnership was less visible in lean times. Furthermore, it had components that had been justified independently for reasons in addition to PNGV, making it more difficult to single out for special attention.

Eager, Highly Motivated Industry Partners

The partners' strongest motivations appear to be both at the highest level and at the working level of the auto industry. The chief executives of each of the Big Three have recognized the benefits of working in partnership with government to address societal issues involving automobiles rather than continuing the confrontational approach that characterized the past decades. At the working level, industry engineers believe they are riding the wave of the future; the new technologies they are evaluating, developing, and incorporating in experimental vehicle designs will, in large part, show up on America's highways within a generation.

Support for the partnership was not universal, however. Industry representatives at the senior leadership and technical levels often found themselves assuming a role as a champion for PNGV within their own corporations. The reasons for less-than-full support for the partnership appeared to spring from a range of causes: reluctance to work with competitors, initial resistance to entering a mutually trusting relationship with government partners, the "not invented here" syndrome (lack of interest because the project was initiated outside the firm), and the simple inertia often characteristic of a large corporation involved in a new enterprise. However, the bulk of the evidence indicates that, over time, PNGV has grown to be generally perceived as offering benefits to industry that outweigh the costs.

Strong Public Interest and Support

This country's love affair with the automobile appears to continue unabated. This, combined with a natural curiosity about new things, has evoked a positive response from public. After a mixed initial reaction to the announcement of the PNGV, the automotive trade press has been a key supporter of the partnership and its goals. The turnaround of the attitude in Congress toward PNGV may, to some degree, be attributable to this interest on the part of the public—combined, of course, with the recognition of the substantial position the automobile industry holds in the U.S. economy.

Effective Technology Transfer

Because the government's scientists are dealing directly with the ultimate user of their technology, the effectiveness of its transfer is increased substantially. The auto industry engineers are able to indicate what aspect of the technology is of greatest interest and where additional research is needed. Such a close match of government and industry technologists is rare. Both parties have benefited from the relationship; the government scientist is exposed to the realities of the industrial world; and the industry engineer gains an appreciation for the breadth of knowledge that may be brought to bear on a problem.

PNGV'S PROBLEM AREAS

PNGV has also encountered certain problems. These have not been insuperable obstacles; rather, they are aspects that complicated the managing of the partnership.

Voluntary Nature of the Commitment

No party in PNGV—on either the government or industry side—is compelled to do anything; all actions are on the basis of "best efforts." As an example, the primary goal, which is widely understood to be 80 miles per gallon is, in fact, "up to 80 miles per gallon." This fine distinction allows the auto industry to settle on the best balance of fuel efficiency, reduced emissions, and affordability. However, the effect of this is to keep interested parties in suspense until September 29, 2003, the end of the partnership. At that time, we will learn how close the industry came to meeting the goals of the program. Until then, the program must rely on the good intentions and commitment of the industry management. This is not meant to imply that the industry is not strongly motivated to participate in the partnership and pursue its goals.

The voluntary aspect was a problem at times with government agency support as well.[25] In spite of the high-level support and

---

[25]For a discussion of why the government agencies and the OEMs—Chrysler, Ford, and General Motors—did decide to participate in the partnership, see "Motivation for the Partnership," above.

leadership described above under Advantages, some participating agencies did not always commit their resources fully to the President's PNGV initiative. The first NRC peer review report was quite direct in addressing this problem, naming several agencies considered to be recalcitrant (NRC, 1994). As the program proceeded, this problem eased considerably.

There were several reasons for this. First, the NRC report, by highlighting the problem, motivated White House officials to bring the problem to the appropriate levels in the uncommitted agencies. Ways in which the agencies might increase their support of the partnership without feeling they were violating their charters were worked out. Second, as the program proceeded, the initial skepticism about the feasibility of achieving the technical goals receded. At the same time, the benefits to the agencies of the automobile companies' success in advancing technologies became more important.

As an example, NASA is constrained to confine its research to technologies related to its mission, aeronautics and astronautics. The auto manufacturers have been interested in expanding the use of aluminum in their vehicles. This promises improved manufacturing techniques and vehicle characteristics. When good prospects emerged in the automotive industry for treating the problems of cost and aluminum joining, NASA became very interested in this activity. Such improvements also hold potential benefits for the aircraft industry. This, and research in other, similar areas of mutual interest led to a more collaborative spirit of partnership by that agency.

So, in future partnerships of this sort, where voluntary commitment is a necessary evil, considerable missionary work will be necessary. Key people in participating agencies must be apprised of the partnership's goals and the part their agency is expected to play. If recalcitrance is experienced later, advocacy must be escalated until a responsive organizational level is reached.

Why was there such a loose arrangement with the PNGV? There were two considerations: First, there were widespread reservations within the automobile industry about meeting what were considered the very challenging PNGV goals. Qualifiers were inserted in the agreement, the most notable of which is the "up to" 80 miles per gallon, to convey some of the sense of a best-efforts approach. Further, there was a wish to avoid the flavor of a requirement or mandate; no party has signed the agreement.

Second, there was the feeling that developments would not proceed in a linear or even an incremental fashion. Therefore, they would not easily be programmable (this, in fact, proved to be the case; very little overall progress was noted in the program until about four years had elapsed). At this point the technical accomplishments came close to final targets.

Therefore, a consequence of the voluntary nature of the partnership is a lack of standard contractual methods. Without these contracts, there has been no model to guide how best to motivate industry in this new and evolving form of organization. Similarly, few government managers had experience operating in a partnership environment that relied less on detailed periodic reports, schedules, or other typical methods for monitoring performance.

Lack of Interim Metrics or Checkpoints

With the exception of commitments to complete a technology-selection process by the end of calendar year 1997 and to build concept vehicles by the year 2000, there are no interim PNGV schedule checkpoints or associated accomplishment metrics. This obviously makes it difficult to assess progress. Goal 2, "Implement commercially viable innovations from ongoing research in conventional vehicles," clearly had midterm accomplishments in mind. In fact, there have been a considerable number of accomplishments (USCAR, 1996). However, the lack of overall quantitative targets as the program progresses, among other things, makes it difficult to convey progress to the public.[26]

Lack of Central Budget

As discussed below in "Budgetary Approach," the government side of the partnership was constrained to operate without a single, dedi-

---

[26]Further discussion of the potential benefit of *not* defining quantitative technical targets from the outset is found in the Trinkle dissertation. Briefly stated, the early definition of restrictive objectives can reduce the flexibility of the technical leadership to define appropriate objectives as the maturing partnership provides better understanding of the problems and the possible technologies to solve them.

cated source of funding for practical reasons. Although there was an advantage to having diverse funding sources, as noted above, the lack of a central budget was a real handicap overall; the principal drawback was an inability to apply additional resources to promising technical developments. Opportunities of this sort would generally necessitate moving funds from the DoC to another agency. A vigorous, technically based, multiagency partnership should be able to do this if it wishes to exploit opportunities. Substantial funds would not be required because, in most cases, incremental increases would be all that is needed to accelerate the project until the regular source of funding could be increased.

Large Number of Parties Involved

Three major domestic automobile manufacturers and seven federal agencies with their 20 laboratories make up a very large technical community. This community must recognize, support, and strive for common goals. Schedules, distribution of tasks, policy positions, and technical solutions must be agreed upon through consensus. All this takes time and effort. The process is in direct contrast to developing a system under government contract, where funding levels, schedule, and a myriad of details are all spelled out before work begins under a binding contract.

Relatively Inflexible Plan

This is generally true of all government enterprises. Because of the lead times involved in the budget process, there is often up to a three-year gap between plans and execution. In many cases in PNGV, new developments would benefit from additional funding. There are also developments that, earlier, were promising but have now lost their luster. Yet, by law, only 10 percent of appropriated R&D funds may be redirected without congressional approval. Such approval usually takes at least six months and is never assured.

Chapter Three

LESSONS LEARNED

> Draw from others the lesson that may profit yourself.
>
> —*Terence*, The Self-Tormentor, *150 BC*

The PNGV still has not reached its halfway point. This exposition on "lessons learned" must be conditioned on its having been drawn from experiences in the early stages of the partnership.

However, the maxim "as the twig is bent, so shall the tree grow" certainly applies in this case. The framework of the program, the organization and content of the program plan, and many other organizational details were negotiated at length within the government and within the industry.[1] The primary reason, I believe, was that the process of renegotiation was found to be so protracted and, in some cases, so agonizing that it was not worth any marginal gain to reopen an issue.

As noted below, Vice President Gore maintained continual interest and made contact with key people. He was instrumental in persuading the auto industry executives. The discussions appear to have used a carrot-and-stick technique. There was of course a realization that what was being proposed represented an opportunity for the industry to set a new course in their relations with the government.

---

[1] This process was described in the "Motivation for the Partnership," above.

More important, for the technically minded industry vice presidents involved in the detail negotiations, there was the lure of new or different kinds of technologies in a new generation of vehicles—the prospect of being a world technology leader. Once they became convinced that the PNGV goals were achievable and that the partnership might work, the vice presidents had to ensure that their organizations would respond positively. This called for them to assume the role of advocate—issuing directives would not be sufficient. Because the partnership has functioned well, we can assume that the vice presidents were convincing in their missionary role. Once established, procedures were not generally tampered with. So, lessons learned during the formative and early stages of the partnership may be said to apply at least through the program's midpoint. Whereas the observations in the following section are specific to PNGV, the lessons learned described below are believed to have pertinence to any future government-industry partnership.

These lessons have been distilled by the author from views expressed by participants in the partnership, primarily but not exclusively on the government side. They more nearly represent personal assessments by seasoned managers than any extensive analytical effort. They could very well be categorized as thoughts on "If We Had To Do It Again."

The essence of this report and the specifics of the observations and lessons learned were presented several times to such groups as OSTP's Committee on Industrial Technology and others concerned with government-industry partnering. Their comments have been factored into this report.

The lessons have been grouped according to the themes underlying each.

STRUCTURING A PARTNERSHIP

Clear and Simply Stated Goals

Clear and simply stated goals are most effective for motivating technical staff and winning public support. "Clean Car" and "80 miles per gallon" are expressions readily understood by the public. Such simply expressed goals also help motivate even the most technically sophisticated scientists. Certainly, there must be well-defined, detailed objectives below that level. But overall, the most useful image in gathering support for PNGV has been of a fuel efficient, environmentally friendly family sedan. This image is easily visualized and thus more likely to be supported by the average person.

High-Level Support

High-level support is vital, within both government and industry. As with any advanced technology project, the interest and support of top management are important for encouraging support within the organization. Given the large number of parties involved and interested in PNGV—within the government, industry, Congress, the media, and the public—high-level political support was imperative. Fortunately, President Clinton considered PNGV to be his initiative, spoke at several key public events, and was consistent in his support. Vice President Gore maintained continual interest and contact with key people. He was the sponsor of a series of vice presidential symposiums on advanced automobile technologies. As of this writing, six have been held. The Vice President has spoken to the participants at all of them. In addition, he and his wife have hosted a reception at their home for the symposium participants.

In a more substantive way, the Vice President and his staff intervened at critical junctures of the program to keep the partnership on track. One of the practical tools available to a government program manager is the prerogative of drawing upon such high-level support as this. Within the government, there was generally no problem enlisting support from working-level managers in participating agencies. However, the curse of government is the many layers of oversight and the large number of people on the periphery of any enterprise. For a range of reasons, some prudent, others less admirable, these conditions offset the worker-level enthusiasm and resulted in the slow progress often characteristic of all large organizations.

On the industry side of the partnership, inaction appeared more rooted in unease about how top management might view certain decisions to collaborate with competitors or with the government. The competitors, it was feared, might learn precious, proprietary secrets. The government, on the other hand, upon learning that something was technically feasible, might mandate it.

In overcoming this inertia, Vice President Gore was especially effective. "Jawboning" is the term generally applied to earnest, but friendly, persuasion. Industry leaders, as well as government officials, find it difficult to resist logical arguments from the Vice President of the United States that they act in the nation's interest. Without these demonstrations of support, the PNGV "success" to date might have been quite a different story.

Of course, the White House cannot become involved in every crisis in every program. Managers must be careful to reserve top-level attention for issues that cannot be resolved in any other way. Technology initiatives, by their nature, give rise to a large number of technical disagreements. These are best dealt with by direct interchange at the working level. Resort to higher-level intervention should be saved for truly important issues.

As seen from the government side, support by industry management was similarly strong and very visible. On numerous occasions, the chief executive officers (CEOs) of Chrysler, Ford, and General Motors have each endorsed the partnership, its goals, and its concept of government-industry collaboration. These are indications that, internal to each of the Big Three firms, this involvement of management was a prize won in hard-fought battles by those industry representatives to the partnership that championed the cause.

Accountability at a High "Politico" Level

Accountability at a high politico level in each participating agency is a must. *Politico* in this case refers to a political appointee, usually a presidential appointment. Individuals in these positions are expected, among their other responsibilities, to ensure that administration initiatives receive full support within their agency. Without such accountability, the extent to which altruistic cooperation may be expected from within an agency is rather limited. Career civil servants are generally reluctant to take initiatives if they fear their leadership might disapprove. Further, people at the technical-team level in almost all cases cannot commit or redirect significant agency resources. This must occur at the politico level—in the case of PNGV, with the Operational Steering Group.

Conversely, if participation in an initiative might confer distinction on an agency, if high-level contacts materialize for managers, and if collaborative efforts are encouraged and recognized within the organization, enthusiasm can know no bounds.

Accountability at a high level is needed also for more pragmatic reasons; technical projects do not always run smoothly. Conflicts arise and adjustments will be necessary. There is also a tendency for some bureaucrats to agree to almost anything in a meeting only to forget the commitment when they leave. In these cases, someone in a position of authority above the working level is needed to keep things on even keel. Also, on happier occasions, a politico would determine who should be recognized for their contributions to the program and what form the recognition should take.

The lesson here is that the pertinent government politicos should be kept involved in the partnership; day-to-day oversight is not required, but a continual awareness of major issues and needs is certainly necessary.

Limited Number of These Kinds of Government-Industry Partnerships

The number of these kinds of government-industry partnerships should be limited. The approach PNGV took was to capitalize on ongoing government research. In many cases, the research was modified or redirected to support the goals of the partnership. This entailed considerable discussion and negotiation and the involvement of key people in many agencies. As may be well-imagined, if, say, a dozen managers of presidential initiatives or similar partnerships were involved with these agencies simultaneously, the climate in the affected research agencies would be very disruptive .

Fortunately, OSTP (in the Executive Office of the President) recognized this potential problem, and the number of government-industry partnerships has been limited to a manageable number.

Anticipation of Funding and Technology Needs

The government must anticipate funding and technology needs at the outset. This is particularly difficult for any government activity but very necessary. It is a true test of the intent and commitment of the government as a partner. Significant delays can sour relations and make proceeding on an orderly basis very difficult.

The approaches considered early in the partnership for more imme-diate funding are discussed in subsections below. None of these were completely satisfactory, which is a problem that persists to some extent today.

The PGNV government manager's approach to funding, as noted earlier, was to capitalize on existing, ongoing research, with the expectation of research redirection and budget augmentation. While redirection occurred in some agencies, it did not occur to the extent originally anticipated. The administration requested an augmented budget, but Congress largely did not grant it.

The first attempt at identifying technology resources was an "inventory" of research projects in each participating agency and laboratory. The product was a ponderous accumulation of paper containing detailed descriptions of specialized research. This was delivered to the industry, whose technologists eagerly awaited the information.

Disappointment and frustration ensued as industry engineers had great difficulty interpreting the often arcane "governmentese" pro-ject descriptions. This was developing into a major impasse when, as an alternative, it was decided to embark on a series of visits to the national laboratories.

The format evolved as the visits proceeded on roughly a once-a-month schedule. The visits emphasized personal interactions between government scientists and industry engineers.

Before a visit, the laboratory management was asked to identify proj-ects they believed were relevant to PNGV goals. Conversations with industry representatives and the PNGV Secretariat translated this into an agenda for the visit.

There was an immediate positive result; for the projects briefed, industry engineers were able to decide their usefulness on the spot and arrange follow-on dialogue.

The downside of the lab visits as a technology-transfer mechanism was that they took over two years to complete. Midway through this process, a new programmatic resource became available—the RaDiUS database. Its objectives closely matched PNGV's needs: It provided a concise description of science and technology projects within or supported by the federal government. The database could be queried using key words or phrases and greatly eased the interpretation problem for the PNGV technical teams.

There was in many instances, nevertheless, continuing difficulty in understanding what the database yielded. In some cases, this was a consequence of indecipherable technical terminology; in other cases, imprecise keywords had been used for the data query.[2] The solution to this was to assign a RAND expert to the technical team to assist with its data searches. So, the lessons in this case are the following:

- identify prospective government research projects early using the RaDiUS database

- assign a database expert to guide the industry users

- embark on a series of visits to laboratories or contractors' sites so that industry engineers may meet, face to face, with government scientists to discuss technology projects of interest.

Problems Associated with the Lack of a Central Budget

Means must be found to surmount problems associated with the lack of a central budget. As explained earlier, utilizing ongoing research permitted a quick start to the partnership. However, the downside of such an approach was the lack of a discretionary, central program budget.

The first NRC peer review report strongly recommended a central budget for the PNGV (NRC, 1994). There are several reasons this proved infeasible. Principally, the problem was that the research activity being drawn upon in the original eight agencies and 19 national laboratories was supported by 12 separate funding sources, six each from House and Senate appropriations bills. Assuming control of these or even redirecting portions of the research might result in activity contrary to that authorized by Congress.

---

[2]The importance of descriptive keywords became evident: Too often, the description pertained to the agency or laboratory mission rather than to the material, process, or technology being investigated.

Other approaches were considered but never implemented. These included a surtax on the R&D budgets of the participating agencies. Because this might result in funds being transferred from one agency to another[3] and thus might raise authorization issues with Congress, it was not adopted. Another mechanism discussed was internal deferral of agencies' funds for research related to the PNGV. The agencies' research plans would be reviewed by the PNGV Secretariat, and the funds would be released when the activity was in accord with the program plan. This approach was considered overly bureaucratic and time consuming.

The upshot was that central technical management of PNGV was primarily effected by suasion. Although this generally worked reasonably well, it was dependent in many cases on the best intentions of people in working environments remote from the PNGV and its goals.

We did consider it extremely important to be able to shift funds within a budget category from less important projects to ones considered to have higher priority. Thus, within a given technology area, say batteries or fuel cells, we were able to adjust to research progress—or lack thereof.

However, the ability to respond quickly to potential breakthrough opportunities has eluded us. Steady support of CRADAs in the national laboratories has also been a problem.[4]

In retrospect, it would have been wise to have requested a modest amount of funding for a central budget. This would be a discretionary source of funds that could be applied to "gap filler" research opportunities until more-traditional funding sources could be tapped. An annual budget of roughly 5 percent of the roughly $300 million PNGV funding level (or about $15 million) would have made a tremendous difference in the ability to manage the government's PNGV research more rationally.

------

[3]Funds may be transferred from one agency to another as long as their purpose is related to the missions of both agencies. Laboratories of the National Institute of Standards and Technology, for example, have received a significant portion of their funding from other federal agencies to develop technologies needed by the funding agencies.

[4]For a description of a DoE–industry partnership that was pursued under a CRADA with several national laboratories, see Lepkowski (1997).

Another reason it would have been wise to have requested a modest amount of funding immediately is that it would have involved Congress earlier. The task of building broader public support would then, by necessity, have been addressed sooner.

Dual-Use Multiagency Projects

Outside of the core program, multiagency projects should be structured for dual use. *Dual use* is defense terminology for an item with both military and civilian applications. By developing working relationships with industries producing knowledge fitting this description, the Department of Defense capitalizes on common research interests. The government's and the contractors' research budgets may thus be extended by leveraging cost-shared joint government-industry research projects.

In the case of the PNGV, the only agency whose mission-oriented research approximates PNGV goals is the DoE. All the other participating federal agencies and laboratories have mission requirements for their research, which only partially overlap the PNGV's technical needs. In supporting the partnership by addressing key PNGV research needs, the participating agencies must find something of value for their missions in automotive technology research. NASA, for example, uses flywheels in several space applications, principally for platform stabilization, and is interested in extending the service life of flywheel bearings. This corresponds to the PNGV's potential need for a highly reliable flywheel for energy storage. Other examples of PNGV-pertinent research include transmissions for armored vehicles, power electronics for ships' electrical systems, and fuel cells for military satellites. Each case represents a dual-use approach to research.

Building on an Existing Core Government R&D Program

It is helpful to build the partnership around an existing core government R&D program. In the case of the PNGV, this was the DoE's Transportation Technologies program. Without such a "running start," the PNGV would have required at least a year, and probably more like two years, to reach the level of activity attained in its first year.

Creating a new partnership without tapping into an existing program involves developing a program plan, determining funding needs, inserting the funding request into the nearest budget request, and then responding to congressional action. In the case of the PNGV, it may have been possible initially to submit a supplemental request for FY94. This might have led to funds being available by the fall of 1994, about a year after the partnership was announced. More likely, a request could have led to funding available in late 1995.

In fact, the first year targeted for a comprehensive PNGV budget request was FY96. This was a consequence of the need to determine how much funding for research was needed in addition to that already programmed and being drawn upon to support the partnership. The planning and analysis behind budget requests are necessary parts of the government's research process. Thus, being able to capitalize on ongoing research can lead to great savings in time and effort.

SOCIAL AND CULTURAL CONSIDERATIONS

Differing Agendas

Although government and industry may agree to pursue the same goals, the agendas should be expected to vary. There is a Japanese saying "same bed, different dreams," that pertains here: There should not be excessive dismay if one or more car companies, government agencies, or national laboratories take some independent initiative. As long as such actions address one or more goals, the partnership will benefit in the long run if the program management is insightful and flexible enough.

Besides pursuing goals related to their missions, government agencies are generally strongly motivated to expand the scopes of their charters. New missions, or extensions of an existing mission, ensure that the agency is meeting public needs; is at the forefront of technology; or, on a more mundane level, has a strong claim for congressional appropriations.

Individual agendas come into play also in large industrial organizations when managers act for self-aggrandizement rather than for the announced policies of the company. Or it may be that, in the absence of firm direction, a subunit follows a course that is at variance with a firm's overall objectives.

It is important to recognize this phenomenon. Otherwise, much energy may expended in appealing to higher interests when all that is needed is finding constructive ways of satisfying less-exalted motives. For example, inviting key undecided people to one of the PNGV receptions at the Gore residence did wonders for developing an appreciation of the value of belonging to the PNGV community. That experience converted many of the uncommitted. They came to appreciate that special status had been conferred on them, and in most cases, they became supporters of the partnership.

Channeling Competition

Competition in industry is a stronger force than cooperation and should be channeled rather than discouraged. Numerous competitive activities advanced the goals of the partnership. Primarily, these involved "packaging" new technologies in concept or experimental vehicles to evaluate their practicality. Although the specifics of an application may have been proprietary, the experience gained and the general evaluation of a new technology quickly become common knowledge within the industry.

Thus, a "keeping up with the Joneses" in the exploration and evaluation of new technologies took place in a competitive environment. A sort of healthy tension arose. At the same time, the PNGV objective of enhancing the overall competitiveness of the domestic automobile industry was advanced.

Social Encounters to Improve Working Interactions

Social encounters improve working-level technical interactions. As mentioned in "Personal Observations" above, there was considerable unease within the auto industry about working with the government. During initial meetings, government and industry representatives dealt warily and only correctly with each other.

Although visits to the national laboratories were organized primarily to highlight research projects that were thought to apply to PNGV, another benefit was noticeable: As industry engineers mixed with government laboratory scientists, technical interests predominated, inhibitions receded, and close personal relationships developed. This was enhanced further by scheduling a reception in the evening between two-day laboratory visits.

Although the monthly laboratory visits ultimately stretched over a two-year period, the social atmosphere described developed within a few months. This led to continuing direct contacts (as opposed to those made through the respective organization's chain of command) and an environment where technical issues were addressed immediately, with all the experts, both government and industry, fully engaged.

Sheltering Technical People from Political Turbulence

Technical people should be sheltered from political turbulence. There was an increasing tendency to involve the technical team in issues that were beyond their experiences, interest, and competence. This usually pertained to a search for government funding for additional research. The effect of this was to divert them from their primary tasks—the ones in which they were valid experts. Turning technical people on and off upsets them and disrupts the project schedule.

The technical challenge has been daunting enough for the technical teams; funding questions invariably had a political overtone that was distracting and frustrating to the technologists. Such concerns should more appropriately have been handled by the management of the partnership.

EXTERNAL ASPECTS

Involving Congress

Program managers must take sufficient time to involve Congress without inviting micromanagement. This situation was a bit of a dilemma from a program-management standpoint. Initially, the Democratic Congress expressed no substantial opposition toward the PNGV, and we therefore saw no pressing need to expend much energy keeping Congress informed. However, as noted earlier, the new Congress initially exhibited hostility toward the project. Shortly after the new Congress was installed, I received a call from a congressional staffer. He said he was having trouble finding either authorization or appropriation language for the PNGV. He needed that information—he said rather baldly—because his boss wanted to kill the program. Up to that point, there had been dismay because the PNGV did not have a central budget, but this diversity of funding sources proved to add a robustness to the program that was hard to foresee. Since each component of the program had been initiated on its own merits and included justification in addition to the contribution made to PNGV, such a narrowly focused challenge along political lines was unpersuasive to the full Congress, which considers a broad range of factors in its resource allocation decisions.

While managing such challenges, we gave a series of briefings to a number of key congressional staffers on the partnership, its workings, and its goals. It was apparent immediately that briefers from industry were perceived as more credible by congressional staffers. The industry engineers talked about research on tangible things, such as engines, transmissions, and batteries and how they would be assembled in future vehicles. By contrast, the government bureaucrats tended to talk about the PNGV organization, budgets, and schedules—relatively dry stuff. So, pride being subordinate to keeping the program alive, the government side of the partnership agreed that the technical briefings to congressional staff should be handled by industry.

As a consequence of a peer review recommendation, the partnership embarked on a broad-based public-affairs effort to explain the program and its goals, benefits, and needs (see the next subsection). The cumulative affect of this, finally, was a congressional endorsement of the partnership (U.S. House of Representatives, 1996). Without such an effort, the PNGV might not be continuing today toward its goals.

The Importance of Public Affairs

Public affairs should be given priority as an extremely important component of a government-industry partnership. As implied above, Congress responds to public impressions of government programs. When new initiatives are announced, there always seems to be an advocacy group somewhere to offer criticism—regardless of

how well-informed they are about the program. This was true originally and continues to be the case for recent PNGV developments.
For example, the announcement of the experimental fuel cell car, the
new internal combustion engine concept, and other new technology
developments all promised dramatic improvements; nevertheless,
they were met with negative comments in some quarters. Initially,
we were quick to rebut an expert's criticism. With time, it appeared
that the public was more interested in the PNGV's latest technical
innovations; the naysayers did not seem to have much lasting influence.[5]

Because of this contentious environment, it is important that any
new initiative create and communicate its message as early as possible in its formative stage. This must be followed by a continued
campaign with the relevant industry press and associated media,
managed by a full-time public-affairs specialist. The technical program managers must be available for such public-affairs campaigns.

PNGV found media events at national laboratories especially effective in conveying information on important aspects of the partnership. These were dedicated to manufacturing (at Los Alamos
National Laboratory in New Mexico), to energy storage (at Sandia
and at Livermore National Laboratory in California), and to materials
(at Oak Ridge National Laboratory in Tennessee). Automotive
reporters were invited to these events and were briefed on key
research projects. They also were able to interview the project scientists for in-depth coverage. The result was numerous articles and
editorials strongly supporting the partnership's research program.

Flexible and Proper Planning for Meeting the Unexpected

Flexibility and proper planning will help when faced with the
inevitable unexpected circumstances. Partnerships with fairly long
time spans will need to allow for flexibility. In the early days of the
PNGV, it was important to prepare and publish a program plan and
certain other planning documents. Not surprisingly, a number of

---

[5]An article in the January 1997 issue of MIT's *Technology Review* is a recent example
(Field and Clark, 1997). A number of erroneous statements about the PNGV led to a
flurry of letters to the editor. Four of the letters were printed in the May/June 1997
issue.

situations arose that were not anticipated in the plans. For example, the substantial investment in research for batteries (see "The Auto Industry Faces a Dynamic Technical Environment," below) for all-electric vehicles was considered a resource for PNGV. As the energy storage problem for hybrid vehicles was analyzed, it became clear that *high-power* batteries were needed rather than the high-energy batteries developed for electric vehicles. A fundamental restructuring of the PNGV's battery-development program therefore became necessary.

At this stage of the partnership, a number of unanticipated developments have occurred in the business realm. Some of these are discussed earlier in this report. Others, quite recent, relating to business deals and developments, may have significant impacts on the PGNV.

With the foregoing as examples, it therefore is important to establish close personal relationships in the early days of the partnership. These most certainly will be drawn upon when the surprises occur.

Chapter Four

OBSERVATIONS

You can observe a lot by just watching.

—*Yogi Berra*

The PNGV currently involves approximately 300 technical people on the government side; somewhat more in the OEMs; and several hundred individual inventors, people in supplier firms, and others in universities. So, to an order of magnitude, about 1,000 scientists and engineers are engaged in the PNGV program. While this is not a huge number of people in the area in which they are engaged, this represents a substantial commitment by both the government and the industry. Further, because these scientists are evaluating and developing new technologies for future vehicles, their potential influence can be substantial.

In observing the evolution of the partnership, certain attitudes, apprehensions, misconceptions, aspirations and mixed feelings became evident to me as the government's technical manager of PNGV. Impressions are, by their nature, personal; others may have seen things differently and may have additional thoughts. My observations, which follow, are specific to PNGV and probably could not be generalized to future partnerships in every instance. However, future managers of government-industry partnerships should be alert to reactions to management directions that appear to be irrational or contrary to agreed objectives. These generally are rooted in institutional cultures or earlier formative experiences. Even though such attitudes are subjective, they must be recognized and addressed if a partnership is to function effectively.

THE AUTO INDUSTRY FACES A DYNAMIC TECHNICAL ENVIRONMENT

There has been very little true invention under the PNGV; on the other hand, there has been considerable reappraisal, redirection, improvement, and unique application of existing systems and technology. Without question, there has been a successful balance between research activities and development efforts.

In the energy storage area, for example, the thinking about the way in which batteries might be used has changed. This has led to a change in the focus of battery development. The initial view was that the PNGV might lead to an electric-powered car with a small engine as a supplement. This "range-extender" configuration would require batteries with an energy content of 6 kilowatt-hours, which meant a substantial weight addition. Because it was assumed that the requirements for pure-electric vehicles and for the PNGV care were similar, research focused on maximizing energy storage.

Several realizations changed that view:

1. Progress on reduction of noxious emissions from energy converters meant that the primary propulsion mode did not have to be electrically driven.

2. The lack of significant progress in improvements in energy density meant that there would be a severe weight penalty with a large battery installation.

3. The most promising high-energy batteries were inherently expensive because of the high cost of critical materials.

4. The batteries being given priority in development for pure electric drives did not handle power (specifically, high currents) very well. They also did not stand up well to the repeated charge and discharge operations of the contemplated PNGV hybrid propulsion system.

After less than a year from the inception of PNGV, but after the PNGV *Program Plan* had been issued, battery research was redirected.

Emphasis was placed on power handling and on extended cycling ability. Meanwhile, analyses of propulsion systems led to significant downscaling of the stored energy requirement, as well as to a redefinition of the operational mode. A "power-assist" hybrid configuration emerged that was considered more compatible with consumer driving patterns. In this arrangement, an engine is the primary propulsion mechanism, assisted as necessary by an electric motor. As a consequence, the energy storage requirement dropped by about an order of magnitude, to 300–500 watt-hours.

Several aspects of high-power batteries warrant continued research, most notably current-carrying ability and cost. However, there is now much more optimism about having a viable energy storage system for the PNGV production prototype.

The transformation described above took less than two years to effect. Similar redefinition and redirections have taken or are taking place in energy conversion, alternative fuels, materials, and manufacturing technologies. Such a dynamic technical environment calls for flexible planning and budgeting. This topic was discussed in Chapter Three.

A "HEAD IN THE SAND" ATTITUDE TOWARD TECHNOLOGICAL ADVANCES CAN BE PERILOUS

A (perhaps unique) perspective of American culture is a conviction that, time after time, history has demonstrated that advances in technology will inevitably reshape the world and the society we live in. Evidence underpinning this conviction includes jet engines supplanting piston engines, transistors replacing vacuum tubes, and integrated circuits dominating transistors. We make investment, business, career, and personal decisions relying on this conviction and find it perilous to ignore such a pervasive "force." The technical evidence is mounting that the PNGV production prototype will be much lighter and more fuel efficient, will have substantially less noxious emissions, and will embody other characteristics that represent a step-change improvement over present day automobiles. To their credit, automotive industry engineers have addressed the challenge of new kinds of materials, energy converters, drives, and control devices in a forthright manner. This has resulted from a change in attitude by some "old hands," plus the enthusiasm of a new wave of younger engineers—probably the right combination to develop a product to be offered to the public.

As new technologies allow new approaches to problem-solving that are not possible with traditional approaches, the attitudes of decisionmakers in America will adjust to the dynamic technical environment encouraged by the PGNV. As this happens, those who choose to rely on the old approach to automotive technology are likely to find themselves out of sync with the market and evolving consumer tastes.

THE "WE'RE DIFFERENT" SYNDROME IS WIDESPREAD

During the early, organizing stages of the program, representatives of the automobile companies would frequently make the point that their industry differed from others. In conversations, people from one company would also assert that theirs was quite different from the other two. The suggestion that aerospace technology in particular might be useful in certain automotive applications would draw the response "no way, aerospace is low volume, high cost; automobiles are high volume, low cost. Aerospace technology doesn't apply." In response, we noted that personal computers are also high volume, low cost—surely there was something to learn from that industry? "Sorry, computers don't face the liability we do; that doesn't apply either."

This attitude was not confined to the industry side: Each of the 19 federal laboratories participating in the program wanted it known that they were unique—even though practically every technology being considered for PNGV was under active investigation by at least two laboratories. Further, representatives of the seven agencies in the partnership would expound without much provocation on how their agency was different, pursued R&D differently, etc.

The phenomenon of individuals proclaiming that they are immune from others intruding into their domains by claiming they are different is well known. Phil Condit, CEO of the Boeing Aircraft Company, has often been cited as saying that the most important thing he had learned since becoming CEO was that planes were, in a broad sense, *no different* from other products. He noted that, historically, Boeing has often responded to criticisms or questions about its operations by saying that building aircraft was so complicated that it had to operate differently from other industries. He considered this to be the biggest excuse for not learning ever invented.

Within the partnership, the initial parochial, defensive attitudes receded, and an open, accepting atmosphere emerged in the partnership in a relatively short time. As a result, the products of the partnership will include a substantial number of useful systems, procedures, technologies, and ideas that emanated from the outside the traditional automobile industry.

The point is not that all enterprises are the same. They certainly are different, by necessity, but uniqueness should not be used as an excuse to fend off ways that do not conform to an industry norm when attacking a problem.

TRADITIONAL TECHNOLOGIES ARE UNLIKELY TO SATISFY THE PNGV'S GOALS

In setting goals in individual technology areas, e.g., 40-percent weight reduction and 45-percent efficient energy converters, the PNGV challenged conventional automobile technologies. It is hardly surprising that the automobile industry, with 100 years of experience using existing processes and materials, would display a strong preference for established technologies. The most entrenched of these were steel, internal combustion engines, and gasoline. Steel is widely available, low cost, and readily formed and joined. Internal combustion engines are reliable and well-understood and represent a substantial investment in capital facilities. Gasoline has the highest energy release among fuels, a very low cost, and an extensive in-place infrastructure. Surpassing these represents a formidable challenge. They have benefited from decades of technological improvement and billions of dollars' worth of investment.

In each case, it was easily established that, in their present—and projected—forms, these would not provide the higher performance levels needed to meet the PNGV's goals. This presented a problem, in human terms, for engineers who had devoted a good part of their careers to a technology that was suddenly threatened. Most of the people actively exploring alternatives easily adjusted to the new technical environment. However, within large engineering organizations, especially at the senior (mature) level, a hostility quickly became evident regarding "new-fangled gadgets." This is an unresolved problem; the older engineers remember, and readily recite, all the earlier innovations that were disappointments: the copper-cooled engine, automobile diesels, etc. Because they are in positions of authority, their apprehensions must be addressed.

FOREIGN EMULATION HAS INCREASED THE MOMENTUM OF TECHNOLOGY ADVANCEMENT

This point simply highlights what informed observers have noted: after the U.S. government announced the PNGV with its domestic automobile industry, considerable activity emulating PNGV ensued abroad. The European Economic Community subsequently announced its "Car of the Future" program; Japanese automobile companies, which had enjoyed long-standing research support from their government, devoted considerable resources to hybrid, PNGV-like concept vehicles; and the Korean, French, and Swedish governments have shown intense interest in PNGV.

The effect of all this is to lock the United States into an international race for automobile technology dominance; the research under way will truly lead to a new generation of fuel-efficient, environmentally friendly vehicles. The firms finding ways to package these advanced technologies in configurations that will find market acceptance should enjoy a substantial lead over their competitors. Once embarked on this partnership, we are compelled to carry it to its goals. If we do not, others who are pursuing similar goals will capture the prize. Our auto industry would then have to settle for second-place status in the world market, in a race that we had initiated.

HOW ENDURING IS INDUSTRY COMMITMENT?

As noted above, a large number of industry people are engaged in PNGV activities. However, the Big Three collectively represent a huge industrial sector with hundreds of thousands of employees. One might wonder, therefore, how enduring the present positive orientation of the industry toward collaborative problem solving on environmental, fuel-efficiency, and safety issues might be.

A precise answer to this question is difficult and, in any event, subjective. Observations will have to provide the indicators of what the prospects might be for a continuing productive relationship between the industry and the government and between the industry partners themselves.

The most immediate observation is that the automobile industry has assigned first-rate people to the partnership. In each technical area—materials, manufacturing, propulsion, electrical, etc.—the automobile companies have assigned top people in their fields to the technical teams. There is an ongoing competition within the auto companies for talent to assign to priority projects. The quality of people assigned to the PNGV technical teams is a reassuring indicator of the importance management places on the partnership.

Another encouraging observation is the relaxed atmosphere among the industry people. They are participating in technical team activities as representatives of highly competitive firms. Yet, it may be because the areas of cooperative research are not customer sensitive that they can afford to be congenial.[1] Whatever their underlying feelings, it is evident that the industry people regard their peers with true professional respect. The desire to advance technology for the benefit of consumers appears genuine.

A favorable indicator also is the rate at which the industry is hiring engineering school graduates who have participated in the "Future Car" competitions. Future Car is a DoE-sponsored program under which 12 universities, selected from a large number of candidates, are given new cars by Chrysler, Ford, or General Motors. The cars are modified by students to improve fuel efficiency and emissions. Because of their experience, the students are in demand in the job market. Roughly one-third of the graduates are hired by auto industry firms, about half of whom go to the OEMs.

Finally, the most telling comment on whether the PNGV spirit of government-industry collaboration will endure came from a USCAR official. He said, "in general, the benefits are so obvious to everyone [in the industry] that it is hard to imaging our not continuing."

---

[1]The operating ground rule for USCAR is cooperation on generic, noncompetitive technology: items whose differences a customer would not sense (such as body frame materials) and that therefore would not sway a decision on which car to purchase.

GOVERNMENT IS A DIFFICULT PARTNER FOR INDUSTRY

Considerable apprehension was noted initially on the industry side regarding simply dealing with the government. In a certain sense, this motivated cooperation. Although one OEM had considerable experience with *research* contracts from the government; another had little; and the third OEM, intentionally, had essentially none. Visions of "big, bad government" intruding in the internal functions of the auto companies abounded.

Those concerns abated as individuals on both sides of the partnership learned to work with each other. The immersion in the technical challenge of the PNGV had a lot to do with the submerging of stereotypes.

However, the government had several problems that have persisted through the program. The first is accountability; finding who is in charge or responsible at a given time for some aspect of the government's commitment is frequently a challenge.

The principal, but by no means the only, contentious aspect is funding. As mentioned earlier, the dynamic nature of the technological environment calls for a flexible approach to funding and budget planning. The assumption that additional federal funding would be forthcoming once the initiative was under way proved false.[2] As a result, the research effort has been constrained by the level of resources. Although some organizational changes have helped this situation somewhat, the problem remains to a great extent. Its roots are what make the government a less-than-perfect partner in research partnerships. They lie principally in the lags between

---

[2]This circumstance was very frustrating at first. A program manager has a difficult enough time when full funding resources are available. Without being able to apply the bureaucratic "Golden Rule" ("he who has the gold makes the rules"), it is nearly impossible to get the attention of people and organizations. By necessity, the management focus for the PNGV shifted from a centrally directed program to one drawing on the technological resources of the federal agencies and their labs. This was also frustrating for the industry participants in that they had to deal with many more entities than they had originally envisioned. However, at this point, the diversity of the technologies may be seen as serendipitous. The industry has been exposed to a wider range of new ideas and approaches than it might have otherwise encountered. As elaborated on elsewhere, the diverse funding sources turned out to be a shield from potential budget cutters.

framing a budget and the two to three years before the funding is available; the limited extent to which funds may be redirected in a timely way (a maximum of 10 percent); and the near impossibility of transferring funds from one agency to another.

Additionally, there is a risk in undertaking a multiyear, technically challenging partnership with the government: If the duration spans several election cycles, interminable reviews and suspended budget decisions could disrupt program schedules and disillusion the industry partner.

There are ways around some of these difficulties. For example, a surtax could be imposed on federal civilian R&D, or targeted projects could be deferred until they are aligned with the partnership goals. But, clearly, thought should be given to improving the flexibility of budget mechanisms if government-industry partnering is to be more widely employed.

SIMILARLY, WORKING WITH INDUSTRY POSES CHALLENGES FOR THE GOVERNMENT

The usual image of industry (as opposed to government) is one of a fast-moving enterprise, quick to make decisions and to capitalize on opportunities. In our dealings with individual auto companies, this was generally the case. But even there, significant problems were noticeable in evaluating ideas from nontraditional sources.

However, the biggest problems arose in dealing with the OEMs collectively. First of all, it should be noted that such activity was illegal before 1984. The Sherman Antitrust Act was then amended to permit collaborative activity in "generic, precompetitive research." This led to the formation of USCAR in 1992. USCAR is officially the industry-side partner of PNGV; Chrysler, Ford, and General Motors are the members of USCAR. Enabling legalisms aside, the business of individuals from one OEM working with other OEMs' people was initially uncomfortable, "an unnatural act," as one put it.

In this atmosphere, decisionmaking by the industry has, at times, been agonizingly slow. A layered organization has built up for the oversight of USCAR, ostensibly to facilitate business. The reverse has occurred; issues sometimes become mired over concern about arcane points.

This no doubt is fixable, but as of this writing, no evidence of improvement is in sight.

Chapter Five

CONCLUSIONS

> By three methods we may learn wisdom: First, by reflec-
> tion, which is noblest; second, by imitation, which is easi-
> est; and third, by experience, which is the bitterest.
>
> *—Confucius*

A government-industry technical partnership needs constant attention and support to be successful. This entails attention to technical
developments and their trends and significance; attention to congressional and public relations; attention to relationships with
participating government agencies and with the industry partners;
and finally, the nurturing of personal relationships with key people in
the partnership.

The experiences and lessons learned from the PNGV should provide
guidance for future, similar government-industry partnerships
addressing technological issues. Although the industries and the
technologies involved may be different, such management concepts
as "parallel technological pathways," the technology-selection process, and an independent peer review seem to have worked for the
PNGV. These concepts therefore should prove very useful for a class
of problems that increasingly confront the nation.

The lessons gained from PNGV experience to date relate to the organizing phase, to social and cultural considerations, and to external
aspects. In organizing, it was important to keep goals simple and
understandable by the general public. The support of the highest
levels of the government was instrumental in ensuring continued

agency participation, as was the identification of a high-level political appointee in each participating agency to shepherd the PNGV activities. It was important to move quickly by anticipating technology and funding needs. In addition to having research apply to the PNGV, it was also important to ensure that the research activity was consistent with that agency's mission. With the partnership established, it was wise to avoid dilution of effort by limiting the establishment of additional, similar partnerships.

With regard to social and cultural considerations, there were clear advantages to appropriating an existing, core government R&D effort. Specifically, this was the DoE's Transportation Technologies program. We recognized and accepted that different organizational entities may have different "agendas" while supporting the effort to meet PNGV goals. Similarly, we saw the competitive urge to be irrepressible and a powerful, positive force when channeled to support the partnership. Also, it became very clear in early encounters that means must be found to stimulate personal interactions between people on both sides of the partnership and at all levels—not only was decisionmaking facilitated, but a foundation of trust was built that made addressing future problems less traumatic.

We learned also, almost too late, that attention must be paid to congressional relations; Congress must be kept informed of goals, progress, and anticipated needs. This should be part of a broader public-affairs effort; when the general public became aware of PNGV and was supportive, congressional relations improved. The improved public image actually helped working relationships within the partnership also.

Cooperation with generic, precompetitive technology is the most that should be expected from a government-industry partnership. However, much more is possible. With interactions as widespread as they are for the PNGV it is understandable—and desirable—that business deals and other ventures, even government realignments, may develop from time to time.

Even at a point less than halfway to its conclusion, the PNGV is showing excellent prospects for its ultimate success. In spite of having to work with a "virtual budget" at times, and other tribulations, we were able to overcome early doubts by enlisting industry competitors and federal agencies unused to working with others to collaborate on a common purpose. We learned that a partnership can be very rewarding for all concerned, a win-win experience for the government, the industry, and for the individuals involved. It certainly was for me.

Chapter Six

AFTERWORD

Nothing worth doing is completed in our lifetime.

—*Reinhold Niebuhr,* The Irony of American History, *1952*

I began writing this report in the summer of 1997—a few months after leaving the DoC. At that time, my intention was simply to document the organizing and early operational stages of the PNGV from the government management perspective. I was careful in the earlier text to avoid proclaiming the PGNV a "success" at this point. This was due to the lack of any preset measures of accomplishment as the program proceeded. Also, without having reached even the mid-point of the partnership's effort, it seemed presumptuous to declare victory based only on management accomplishments. However, recent events appear to indicate a higher likelihood of success than previously assumed. Notwithstanding Niebuhr's claim, it seems there are reasons to believe something worth doing will be accomplished well within the lifetime of the PNGV participants.

The following discussion has been added at the urging of the government PNGV participants who reviewed the preliminary draft of the report. This chapter provides details of some of the recent developments relevant to the PNGV effort. The most notable of these is the display by the Big Three of their concept and experimental cars during the 1998 Detroit Auto Show.

RECENT REVELATIONS

Displays by the Big Three auto manufacturers of vehicles incorporating PNGV-sponsored technologies may be seen as an early indication of the ultimate success of the PNGV.

The automobile industry frequently displays "concept vehicles" or experimental cars to test public reaction and determine their marketability. As described in Chapter Two, the 1997 Detroit Auto Show was the first public indication that the Big Three auto companies were seriously considering PNGV-related technologies. However, with the exception of General Motors' EV-1, the experimental cars displayed were a long way from being marketable products.

Although the participants in the PNGV were confident that their research and development would lead to a new vehicle configuration with beneficial characteristics, observers were not so sure. Figure 8

Figure 8—Forecast of the Result of the Partnership

was an early forecast of the outcome of the partnership. Some outsiders thought it to be doomed to be a government bureaucrat's fantasy or the product of a committee with no feel for the market.

In contrast to the cartoon—or even the 1997 Detroit Auto Show displays—the recent 1998 Detroit Auto Show displays by the Big Three were a dramatic advance. Each of the PNGV partners unveiled concept or experimental cars that not only incorporated advanced technologies but also promised dates for market introductions. The vehicles displayed appeared as much as two years sooner than generally expected—a very encouraging sign that the industry partners were making a serious effort.

Chrysler featured its Dodge Intrepid ESX2, a second-generation hybrid concept car "with the potential to meet future emission requirements and achieve 70 miles per gallon." (Chrysler Corporation, 1998.) It incorporated lightweight body technology and a new direct-injected diesel-electric engine in a hybrid drive-train configuration. As compared to many concept vehicles, the ESX2 was actually driven about and was able to operate smoothly in all drive modes. It is shown in Figure 9.

Ford displayed their P2000 DIATA, "a revolutionary family car prototype that gets 63 miles to the gallon." (Ford Motor Company, 1998). The lighter-weight car was equipped with an all-new, 1.2 liter compression-ignition, direct-injection engine in a conventional drive train. Also able to be driven, the P2000 was about the size projected

Figure 9—Dodge Intrepid ESX2

for the PNGV production prototype and met the weight target of 2,000 pounds—40 percent less than today's Ford Taurus. The lightweight materials include aluminum (a major component for the body and engine), carbon fiber, magnesium, and titanium. The Ford P2000 is shown in Figure 10.

At the same time, Jac Nasser, Ford Automotive Operations President, said that "later this year, we'll have an electric hybrid-powered version of the P2000 on the road. And by 2000, we will have a fuel-cell version that produces no emissions other than water vapor."

In December 1997, Ford also announced that it had formed a global alliance to develop fuel-cell technology with Ballard Power Systems of Canada and Daimler-Benz AG of Germany.[1]

General Motors revealed a family of vehicles that included an extended-range, all-electric EV-1; a fuel-cell experimental car; a gas-turbine series hybrid-electric vehicle; and an 80–mile per gallon, all-wheel-drive hybrid performance car (General Motors, 1998). Speaking at the 1998 Detroit Auto Show, John F. Smith, Jr., General Motors CEO, said "we plan to have a production-ready hybrid electric vehicle by 2001 and a fuel cell vehicle by 2004, or sooner." Further, Smith noted that General Motors' strategy of pursuing a family of options provides the most promise of increasing fuel economy and lowering emissions.

However, he cautioned that mandating target emissions levels and dates is risky. "Innovation, not regulation, is the answer to reducing emissions. Regulation can divert an automaker's resources and attention from fully exploring [a] range of technologies. . . ."

General Motors' "Parallel Hybrid Electric" vehicle displayed at the 1998 Detroit Auto Show is pictured in Figure 11. It was described as the world's first eco-friendly hybrid sports car. Its front wheels are driven by an electric motor, the rear wheels by an Isuzu direct-injection turbodiesel. The transmission is an Opel auto-shift manual. An all-wheel drive provides regenerative braking and improved traction. Burning diesel fuel, the car gets 80 miles per

---

[1] "Ford Joins in a Global Alliance to Develop Fuel-Cell Auto Engines" (1997).

Figure 10—Ford P2000

Figure 11—General Motors "Parallel Hybrid Electric"

gallon on the highway driving cycle, has a 550 mile range, and accelerates from 0 to 60 mph in seven seconds.

FOREIGN DEVELOPMENTS

Detroit has not been alone in exploring advanced technologies for automobiles. As noted earlier in this report, foreign auto manufacturers, most notably Japanese and German, have responded to the R&D activities of the PNGV with announcements of their own similar projects.

The compact-class Toyota Prius appears to be Japan's auto industry's most elegant engineering configuration of a hybrid-electric vehicle. Toyota claims that the car achieves an average 66.5 miles per gallon on the Japanese driving cycle with a direct-injection gasoline engine mated with an electric motor.[2] The engine and motor are designed to turn on and off independently for optimum efficiency. Also, energy is regenerated during deceleration and braking to convert the car's kinetic energy into electrical energy.

Honda Motor Company earlier announced a new drive train that included a hybrid engine, a continuously variable transmission, and regenerative braking.[3] Fuel economies in excess of 70.4 miles per gallon of gasoline were claimed for the hybrid power train. A new engine was described, the Honda Integrated Motor assist system, based on a lightweight, three-cylinder, direct-injection engine.

Nissan Motor Company separately revealed work on direct-injection gasoline and diesel engines that give fuel economy improvements of 20 to 30 percent.[4]

In Germany, Daimler-Benz, as noted earlier, announced that it had teamed with Ford and Ballard Power Systems of Canada to begin producing as many as 100,000 cars a year powered by fuel cells by the year 2004.[5] Separately, Volkswagen is experimenting with several configurations of vehicles with hybrid propulsion systems, and Siemens has developed an electric power unit for use in Audi's "duo" hybrid vehicle.[6]

The motivations for all this activity in environmentally friendly, fuel-efficient automobile technology outside the United States may have been reasons other than "keeping up with the Americans," but in any event, the resulting effect is an international race of sorts. As noted in Chapter Three, the competitive urge is very strong in the automobile industry. Management's plans for the PNGV did not necessarily think in terms of an *international* competition. However, the foreign developments described above have certainly intensified the competitive atmosphere.

---

[2] "Toyota's Green Machine" (1997).

[3] "Honda Unveils Advanced Technology" (1997).

[4] "Nissan to Manufacture New Direct-Injection, Diesel, Gas Engines," 1997

[5] "Ford, Daimler-Benz and Ballard Join Forces" (1997).

[6] "Siemens' Electric Powerpoint" (1997).

The relationship of the auto industry in each country with its government is different. The approach the U.S. government took with the PNGV has not been duplicated elsewhere. However, the European Community has formed a "Task Force for the Car of Tomorrow." Its aim is to "contribute to the research and demonstration effort necessary to develop a competitive vehicle that is clean, safe, efficient, and intelligent." (European Community, 1995.)

So, the PNGV is in a race that it appears to have stimulated. The outcome of the race will no doubt be measured in miles per gallon of fuel consumption, grams per mile of emissions, quantities of clean cars produced, and similar numbers. But the answer to the question of how our government should interact best with technology-intensive industries may be found in relevant results of the PNGV experience, especially in increased technological competitiveness.

TECHNOLOGY SELECTION

The recent Detroit Auto Show displays of concept vehicles by the Big Three partners largely reflect the decisions of the technology-selection process. These cars have now been seen, touched, and in some cases, driven by media representatives and government officials. The challenge at this point will be to produce them in quantity, have them meet safety and emission standards, and—the most daunting—reduce their costs to provide an "equivalent cost of ownership."

The primary objective of the technology selection was to narrow the R&D focus by identifying areas where government resources should be concentrated. According to the announcement of the technology selection,

> while the new concepts recently unveiled in Detroit are impressive, significant additional technology breakthroughs and advancements will be required to achieve the ambitious PNGV goals . . . the government partners and their labs . . . will continue to participate in high risk, cooperative research and development with the automobile industry to advance critical enabling technologies for possible use in these vehicles. (DoC and USCAR, 1998).

So an important PNGV milestone has been passed. A key point to appreciate is the effect of the technology selection on government

PNGV managers. They must reallocate resources and justify additional funds to respond to the technology-selection recommendations. This involves trade-offs with other agency priorities, a stressful exercise.

Fortunately, the administration has risen to the challenge (DoC and PNGV Secretariat, 1998). The Fiscal Year 1999 federal budget has requested a 22-percent increase in funding for the PNGV. Technologies designated for increased research support included, primarily, fuel cells, direct-injection engines, advanced fuels, and advanced batteries, all identified by the technology selection. In addition, there is an intention to decrease funding for research—a rare event in government R&D circles—on technologies deemed to be less important. Gas turbines and ultracapacitors were in the latter categories. Less funding was also requested for hybrid vehicle system designs because the industry was moving into more proprietary, commercial applications.

It should be kept in mind that the industry partners are not obligated to incorporate any of these advanced technologies into designs for their production prototypes. Among the technical PNGV goals are producibility, affordability, and safety considerations. When the challenge of balancing these considerations is appreciated, the wisdom of a government-industry partnership becomes more apparent. Both parties have been able to concentrate on what they do best. The incremental cost to the U.S. taxpayers, above the ongoing cost of maintaining the federal R&D establishment, has been minimal. The benefits, on the other hand, should be very substantial in the way of reduced energy consumption, an improving environment, and a technically invigorated, more competitive industry.

A precise determination of the true costs the government incurred with the PNGV would be difficult. The dual-use aspect discussed in Chapter Three, as well as other complications in government accounting, would have to be considered. Similarly, the benefits of the partnership would be hard to quantify. The principal problem would be associated with the lags between the introduction of "clean cars" and when changes in the environment are noticed. Nevertheless, costs may be approximated, and benefits in many areas—such as reduced cost of ownership for car buyers, reduced imports of foreign oil, and a cleaner environment—may be quantified roughly. These, then, may be compared by thorough analysis to determine the value of the PNGV and perhaps set a rough quantitative standard for future government-industry partnerships.

REFLECTIONS

The detachment that has come from being away from active involvement in the PNGV's technical activities has led to some thinking about what may be the most significant aspect of the partnership. The recent developments described above, in particular, have raised in my mind the question of whether meeting specific fuel economy and emissions targets may be the most important result of the PNGV.

It appears there is reasonable assurance of success for the PNGV; the recent announcements by the Big Three OEMs and other indications—mostly from personal conversations with industry managers—are very encouraging regarding the intention of the industry to continue to consider seriously advanced technology.

There could be a debate about what constitutes "success." Most certainly, the car companies will be expected to produce production prototypes by September 29, 2003, that can achieve up to three times the fuel efficiency—80 miles per gallon—performance comparable to 1994 family sedans, reduced emissions, and improved recyclability and also be able to meet federal safety standards and have cost of ownership equivalent to comparable 1994 sedans (as stipulated in the PNGV *Program Plan*).

However, the family sedans were "baselined" originally for the PNGV because at the time they represented the largest segment of the U.S. vehicle market. Since that time, family sedans have become a declining share of the U.S. automobile market. They have been, or are projected to be, supplanted in that position by sport utility vehicles (SUVs) and light trucks. The SUVs are basically trucks from the standpoint of their performance; they consume more fuel and emit greater noxious fumes than present-day sedans—substantially more than is expected from the PNGV's "clean cars."

So, with an increasing number of "gas-hog" SUVs being produced and fewer of the originally projected clean cars expected, have the PNGV's attentions been misplaced?

As pointed out above in "PNGV's Advantages," having a simple goal (80 miles per gallon) was very useful. Initially, the PNGV participants' greatest technical challenge was to develop means to reduce fuel consumption to meet that goal. Today, arguably, their preoccupation is generally considered to be with minimizing emissions, especially particulates.

This is not necessarily a change in priorities; it is more one of resolving pressing technical problems and moving on to the next "blocker." The environment that permits this is one of a continuing review of the state of the art of technologies that have potential for automotive application. So, with the means in hand to reduce vehicle weight substantially while preserving safety features, to improve drive-train efficiency, and to reduce emissions, the industry may apply them to SUVs or other light-duty vehicles as the occasion demands.

The PNGV's technical management on the government side strove from the beginning to create such an environment. The national laboratory visits, all–technical team reviews, and other personal interactions at the technical-team level were seen as the key to effecting a long-term change in the industry's product development philosophy. It will be difficult to define a measure of success for such an undertaking, but in time, it should be seen as one of the most important collateral benefits of a government-industry partnership.

FUTURE DIRECTIONS

The question has been asked: "Should PNGV be extended?" To 120 miles per gallon? To zero emissions? There are reasonable arguments for keeping the teams together and maintaining the problem-solving momentum. On the other hand, if the PNGV observes the "sunset" provision and concludes as scheduled on September 29, 2003, a precedent might be set that the end of a partnership should be a time for assessment. The results, accomplishments, and gaps may then be examined and compared to the original goals. The benefits may then also be compared to the costs to determine the value of the partnership.

With regard to unresolved technical problems or a desire to push on to higher levels of accomplishment, it would seem wise to negotiate a new partnership agreement. This would allow a clear focus on remaining problems and on what the appropriate roles for government and industry should be. It should also yield a better agreement in that the experience with the PNGV would be a guide.

A new agreement could also lead to a rethinking on the government side of how best to support such a partnership. One change that should be considered seriously in future efforts of this kind is a stronger leadership role at the highest levels of the White House. A lead agency for a new partnership is likely to be handicapped just as the leadership in the DoC was by the factors mentioned in "PNGV Problem Areas": lack of a central budget, voluntary commitment on the part of participating agencies, etc.

The OSTP's legislative charter calls for it to "assist the President in providing general leadership and coordination of the research and development programs of the federal government." Future partnerships of this kind would be assured of higher-level attention and quicker response to the complex issues they must face if such leadership were strongly in evidence. This would especially be the case if the government-industry partnership were operating in a constrained-budget atmosphere. Based on the experience of PNGV (e.g., recent budget and personnel reductions, which have limited the ability of the PNGV Secretariat to meet its commitments), this is likely to be the case. As in any complex undertaking, a careful balance will need to be achieved between the operational roles of the lead agency and the leadership role that the White House staff would need to assume for the President in order to manage those problems that can only be effectively addressed above the agency level.

Whatever approach the PNGV takes in the future, it will be likely to have administration support. President Clinton (1998) recently announced a plan to offer a tax credit of $3000 beginning in the year 2000 toward the purchase of

> advanced-technology cars that get more than twice the mileage of today's models—when these cars become even more efficient, we'll increase the tax credit to $4000. We're committed to making it not only wiser, but actually cheaper, to buy highly efficient cars. Working together, we will overcome the challenge of global climate change and create new avenues of growth for our economy. And, most important, we'll honor our deepest responsibility to pass on this home, without harm, to our children, our grandchildren and generations yet to come.

SELECTED COMMENTS ON PNGV

The following editorial commentary generally illustrates the media's changing attitudes toward the PNGV as they evolved from skeptical to more generally supportive.

RESPONSES TO INITIAL ANNOUNCEMENT OF THE PARTNERSHIP

—Max Gates, "Clean-Car Effort Carries Many 'Ifs,'" *Automotive News*, October 4, 1993:

> There are few guarantees in the government-Big 3 agreement, called the "Partnership for a New Generation of Vehicles." The seven-page document is long on good intentions but short on promises, as reflected by its subtitle, "A Declaration of Intent."

—William Safire, "U.S.–Automaker Pact Is Corporate Statism," *New York Times*, October 1993:

> Corporate statism arrived in America last week in the back seat of a dream car. Proponents of today's "partnership" cloak their takeover in the rhetoric of saving on research, promotion of exports, job creation, all those good things competent executives do better than bureaucrats. Ironically, we're aping Japan just when the terrible weakness of the protective Japanese system is becoming manifest.

Bunten, John, *From Confrontation to Cooperation: How Detroit and Washington Became Partners*, Harvard University, C106-97-1382.0, 1996.

Clinton, Bill, Radio Address of the President to the Nation, Washington, D.C.: The White House, January 31, 1998.

Clinton, Governor Bill, and Senator Al Gore, *Putting People First: How We Can All Change America*, New York: Times Books, 1992.

Coburn, Christopher, ed., *Partnership: A Compendium of State and Federal Cooperative Technology Programs*, Columbus, Ohio: Battelle, 1995.

Chrysler Corporation, Press Release, Detroit Auto Show, January 6, 1998.

DoC—*see* U.S. Department of Commerce.

"Effort to Reduce Funds for PNGV a Bad Idea," editorial, *Automotive News*, August 4, 1997.

European Community, Office for Official Publications, "Car of Tomorrow," Luxembourg, 15B 911-827-5386-7, L-2985, 1995.

Executive Office of the President, "Declaration of Intent," September 29, 1993.

Field, Frank R., III, and Joel P. Clark, "A Practical Road to Lightweight Cars," *Technology Review*, January 1997, pp. 28–36.

"Ford, Daimler-Benz and Ballard Join Forces," *PR Newswire*, December 15, 1997.

"Ford Joins in a Global Alliance to Develop Fuel-Cell Auto Engines," *The New York Times*, December 16, 1997.

Ford Motor Company, Press Release, Detroit Auto Show, January 5, 1998.

Gates, Max, "Clean-Car Effort Carries Many 'Ifs,'" *Automotive News*, October 4, 1993.

General Motors, Press Release, Detroit Auto Show, January 4, 1998.

Hebert, H. Josef, "Clinton Unveils Energy Package," Associated Press, February 1998.

Hillebrand, D. H, *Government-Participant Interactions Under the Partnership for a New Generation of Vehicles*, Society of Automotive Engineers, 1996.

Holzman, David, "A Driving Force," *Environmental Health Perspectives*, Vol. 105, No. 6, June 1997.

"Honda Unveils Advanced Technology," *The Wall Street Journal*, September 19, 1997.

House—*see* U.S. House of Representatives.

Kutter, Robert, "Don't Thank the Free Market for Eco-Friendly Cars," *Business Week*, February 16, 1998

Lepkowski, Wilbert C., "AMTEX—A CRADA for all Seasons," *Chemical and Engineering News*, Washington, D.C.: American Chemical Society, November 24, 1997.

"Nissan to Manufacture New Direct-Injection, Diesel, Gas Engines," *The Wall Street Journal*, September 19, 1997.

National Research Council, Board on Energy and Environmental Systems and Transportation Research Board, *Review of the Research Program of the Partnership for a New Generation of Vehicles*, Washington, D.C.: National Academy Press, 1994.

National Research Council, Standing Committee to Review (PNGV), *Research Program of the Partnership for a New Generation of Vehicles: Second Report,* Washington, D.C.: National Academy Press, 1996.

_____, *Research Program of the Partnership for a New Generation of Vehicles: Third Report,* Washington, D.C.: National Academy Press, 1997.

_____, *Research Program of the Partnership for a New Generation of Vehicles: Fourth Report,* Washington, D.C.: National Academy Press, 1998.

NRC—*see* National Research Council.

Safire, William, "U.S.-Automaker Pact Is Corporate Statism," *The New York Times,* October 1993.

"Siemens' Electric Powerpoint . . . ," *PR Newswire,* December 10, 1997.

Stix, Gary, "Pipe Dream: A Consortium Ponders Remaking the Automobile," *Scientific American,* February 1994.

"Supercar Deserves Top U.S. Priority—Like Moon Trips," editorial, *Automotive News,* September 4, 1995.

"Toyota's Green Machine," *Business Week,* December 15, 1997, p. 108.

Trinkle, David, *A Vehicle for Change: The Partnership for a New Generation of Vehicles, An Experiment in Government-Industry Cooperation,* dissertation, Santa Monica, Calif.: RAND, forthcoming.

USCAR—*see* U.S. Council for Automotive Research.

U.S. Congress, Office of Technology Assessment, *Advanced Automotive Technology: Visions of a Super-Efficient Family Car,* 1995.

U.S. Council for Automotive Research, *Mileposts,* Southfield, Mich., published quarterly.

U.S. Council for Automotive Research, *PNGV Accomplishments,* Southfield, Mich., 1996.

U.S. Department of Commerce, *PNGV Program Plan,* revised, Washington, D.C., November 29, 1995.

U.S. Department of Commerce, *Inventions Needed for PNGV,* revised Washington, D.C., August 1996.

U.S. Department of Commerce, PNGV Secretariat, "President Clinton Supercharges PNGV Initiative, Proposes $50 million Boost in R&D on Fuel-Efficient Vehicles," press release, Washington, D.C., January 30, 1998

U.S. Department of Commerce and the U.S. Council for Automotive Research, "PNGV Narrows Focus in National Effort to Develop Advanced, Affordable Automotive Technologies," joint announcement, Washington, D.C., and Southfield, Mich., January 23, 1998.

U.S. House of Representatives, "Partnership for a New Generation of Vehicles (PNGV): Assessment of Program Goals, Activities and Priorities," Hearing before the Subcommittee on Energy and Environment of the Committee on Science on July 20, 1996, Washington, D.C.: U.S. Government Printing Office, 1996.

Womack, James P., Daniel T. Jones, and Daniel Roos, *The Machine that Changed the World: The Story of Lean Production,* Cambridge, Mass.: Harper Perennial, 1990.